50 Fabulous

Pineapple Crochet Motifs

by Jean Leinhauser and
Ferosa Harold

Leisure Arts, Inc.
Little Rock, Arkansas

Produced by

Production Team
Creative Directors: Jean Leinhauser and
Rita Weiss
Technical Editor: Ellen W. Liberles
Photographer: Carol Wilson Mansfield
Book Design: Linda Causee

Published by Leisure Arts

©2010 by Leisure Arts, Inc.,
5701 Ranch Drive
Little Rock, AR 72223
www.leisurearts.com

Introduction

The pineapple has been one of the most popular crochet motifs for well over one hundred years, and is still going strong today.

Aside from its inherent beauty, what else has contributed to its popularity? Probably the fact that since colonial days the pineapple has been a symbol of hospitality.

Although most of us today associate the pineapple with Hawaii, it actually was discovered hundreds of years ago in South America. Its origin was probably Brazil or Paraguay, but it was known throughout the region long before European ships arrived.

When Christopher Columbus landed in what is now Guadalupe on his second voyage to the New World in 1493, we're sure he never would have imagined that images of this pinecone-shaped fruit would one day be flying off the hooks of crocheters! It was considered a rare and delicious delicacy when Columbus brought plants back to Spain.

It reached the shores of the United States in the 17th century when shipping routes from the Caribbean made it possible for wealthy colonists to obtain the exotic fruit and offer it to guests as a special welcoming treat.

The pinecone symbol became so popular that it soon was topping bed posts, newel posts, gates, and wherever else the owner wanted to indicate a sense of welcome and friendship.

That the crocheted pineapple is a versatile design is proven by the 50 motifs in this booklet. The crocheted pineapple turns itself into a peacock, a Christmas tree, an owl and many other unusual designs, as well as appearing in a variety of shapes.

All of our photographed models were made with Size 10 crochet cotton, but you can of course make them in any thread or yarn you choose, so no gauge is given.

Crocheted pineapple projects make wonderful gifts, especially for housewarming events.

Contents

Lovely Pineapple

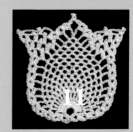

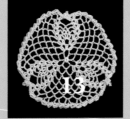

Pineapple Fish

Pineapple Shining Star

Pineapple in Flight

Pineapple Owl

Pineapple Angel

Petite Pineapple

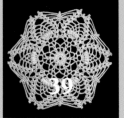

Pineapple Cobweb

Pineapple Basket

Pineapaple Cluny Leaves

Pineapple Peacock

Pineapple Twins

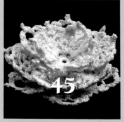

Pineapple Water Lily

Pineapple Lady

Pineapple Triangles

Circle of Pineapples

Pineapple Ring

Marching Pineapples

Pineapple Vase

Pineapple Clusters

Mystical Pineapples

Pineapple Butterfly

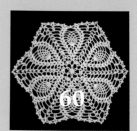

Fancy Pineapples

Posies and Pineapples

Pretty Pineapples

General Directions 65

Lovely Pineapple

STITCH GUIDE

Back Post Slip Stitch (bp sl st): Insert hook from back to front to back around post (vertical bar) of specified st in rnd below, YO and draw through both lps on hook.

Beginning Shell (beg shell): In specified st, work (ch 3, dc, ch 2, 2 dc).

Shell: In specified st, work (2dc, ch 2, 2 dc).

Beginning Double Shell (beg d-shell): In specified sp, work [ch 3, dc, (ch 2, 2 dc) twice].

Double Shell (d-shell): In specified sp work (2 dc, ch 2) twice, 2 dc in same st.

V- Stitch (V-st): In specified st, work (dc, ch 2, dc).

Picot: Ch 3, sl st in first ch made.

INSTRUCTIONS

Ch 6, join with a sl st in first ch to form a ring.

Rnd 1: Ch 3, work 17 dc in ring; join with a sl st in 3rd of beg ch-3: 18 dc.

Rnd 2: Bp sl st in beg dc; *ch 3, bp sl st in next dc; rep from * around, ch 1, join with hdc in first bp sl st.

Rnd 3: Ch 5 (counts as dc and ch-2 sp); *dc in ch-3 sp, ch 2; rep from * around, join with a sl st in 3rd ch of ch 5: 18 ch-2 sps.

Rnd 4: Sl st in ch-2 sp, beg shell in same sp; *ch 1, sk next dc, V-st in next dc, ch 1**, skip one ch 2 sp, shell in next ch-2 sp; rep from * around, end at ** on last rep; join with a sl st in 3rd of ch-3.

Rnd 5: Sl st in dc and ch-2 sp, beg shell in same sp; *ch 2, 5 dc in V-st, ch 2**, shell in shell; rep from * around, end at **on last rep; join with a sl st in 3rd ch of beg ch-3.

Rnd 6: Sl st in dc and ch-2 sp, beg shell in same sp; *working in next 5-dc group (ch 1, dc in dc) 5 times, ch 1**, shell in shell; rep from * around, end at ** on last rep, join with a sl st in 3rd ch of beg ch-3.

Rnd 7: Sl st in dc and ch-2 sp, beg d-shell in same sp; *ch 3, skip one ch-1 sp, (sc in next ch-1 sp, ch 3) 4 times**, d-shell in shell; rep from * around, end at ** on last rep, join with a sl st in 3rd ch of beg ch-3.

Rnd 8: Sl st in dc and ch-2 sp, beg shell in same sp; *ch 3, shell in next ch-2 sp, ch 3, skip one ch-3 sp, (sc in next ch-3 sp, ch 3) 3 times**, shell in next ch-2 sp; rep from * around, end at ** on last rep, join with a sl st in 3rd ch of beg ch-3.

Rnd 9: Sl st in dc and ch-2 sp, beg shell in same sp; *ch 3, sc in ch-3 sp, ch 3, shell in shell, ch 3, skip one ch-3 sp, (sc in next ch-3 sp, ch 3) twice**, shell in shell; rep from * around, end at ** on last rep, join with a sl st in 3rd ch of beg ch-3.

Rnd 10: Sl st in dc and ch-2 sp, beg shell in same sp; *(ch 3, sc in next ch-3 sp) twice, ch 3, shell in shell, ch 3, skip one ch-3 sp, sc in next ch-3 sp, ch 3**, shell in shell; rep from * around, end at ** on last rep, join with a sl st in 3rd ch of beg ch-3.

Rnd 11: Sl st in dc and ch-2 sp, (ch 3, dc, picot, 2 dc) in ch-2 sp; *ch 5, skip one ch-3 sp, (sc, picot, sc) in next ch-3 sp, ch 5, (2 dc, picot, 2 dc) in shell, ch 5, (sc, picot, sc) in sc, ch 5**, (2 dc, picot, 2 dc) in next shell; rep from * around, end at ** on last rep, join with a sl st in 3rd ch of ch-3. Finish off; weave in thread ends.

Pineapple Heart

STITCH GUIDE

Beginning Shell (beg shell): In specified st work (ch 3, dc, ch 2, 2 dc).

Shell: In specified st, work (2dc, ch 2, 2 dc).

Beginning Double Shell (beg d-shell): In specified st work [ch 3, dc, (ch 2, 2 dc) twice].

Double Shell (d-shell): In specified st work [(2 dc, ch 2) twice, 2 dc].

V-Stitch (V-st): In specified st work (dc, ch 2, dc).

Cluster (Cl): (YO insert hook in specified st, YO and draw up a lp, YO and draw through 2 lps on hook) twice; YO and draw through rem 3 lps on hook.

Picot: Ch 3, sl st in last st made.

INSTRUCTIONS

Row 1: Ch 4, work (dc, ch 2, 2 dc) in first ch st; ch 1, turn.

Row 2: Sl st in 2 dc and ch-2 sp, beg d-shell in same sp; ch 1, turn.

Row 3: Sl st in 2 dc and ch-2 sp, beg shell in same sp; ch 3, shell in shell; ch 1 turn.

Row 4: Sl st in 2 dc and ch-2 sp, beg shell in same sp; ch 2, V-st in ch-3 sp, ch 2, shell in shell; ch 1, turn.

Row 5: Sl st in 2 dc and ch-2 sp, beg shell in same sp; ch 2, 5 dc in V-st, ch 2, shell in shell; ch 1, turn.

Row 6: Sl st in 2 dc and ch-2 sp, beg shell in same sp; (ch 1, dc in next dc of 5-dc group) 5 times, ch 1, shell in shell; ch 1, turn.

Row 7: Sl st in 2 dc and ch-2 sp, beg d-shell in same sp; ch 3, skip one ch-1 sp, (sc in next ch-1 sp, ch 3) 4 times, d-shell in shell; ch 1, turn.

Row 8: Sl st in 2 dc and ch-2 sp, beg shell in same sp; ch 3, shell in next ch-2 sp, ch 3, skip one ch-3 sp, (sc in next ch-3 sp, ch 3) 3 times, shell in next ch-2 sp, ch 3, shell in next ch-2 sp; ch 1 turn.

Row 9: Sl st in 2 dc and ch-2 sp, beg shell in same sp; ch 2, V-st in ch-3 sp, ch 2, shell in shell, ch 3, skip one ch-3 sp; (sc in next ch-3 sp, ch 3) twice, shell in shell, ch 2, V-st in ch-3 sp, ch 2, shell in shell; ch 1, turn.

Row 10: Sl st in 2 dc and ch-2 sp, beg shell in same sp; ch 2, 5 dc in V-st, ch 2, shell in shell, ch 3, skip one ch-3 sp, sc in next ch-3 sp, ch 3, shell in shell, ch 2, 5 dc in V-st, ch 2, shell in shell; ch 1, turn.

Row 11: Sl st in 2 dc and ch-2 sp, beg shell in same sp; skip next 2 dc on shell, skip 2 dc, (ch 1, dc in next dc) 5 times, ch 1, shell in shell, ch 2, shell in shell, working on next 5-dc group (ch 1, dc in next dc) 5 times, ch 1, shell in shell; ch 1, turn.

Row 12: Sl st in 2 dc and ch-2 sp, beg shell in same sp; *ch 3, skip one ch-1 sp, (sc in next ch-1 sp, ch 3) 4 times, shell in shell**; ch 2, in ch-2 sp work, (sc, picot, sc), ch 2, shell in shell; rep from *to ** once more; ch 1, turn.

Row 13: Sl st in 2 dc and ch-2 sp, beg shell in same sp; ch 3, skip one ch-3 sp, (sc in next ch-3 sp, ch 3) 3 times, shell in shell; ch 1, turn, leaving rest of row unworked for now.

Row 14: Sl st in 2 dc and ch-2 sp, beg shell in same sp; ch 3, skip one ch-3 sp, (sc in next ch-3 sp, ch 3) twice, shell in shell; ch 1, turn.

Row 15: Sl st in 2 dc and ch-2 sp, beg shell in same sp; ch 3, skip one ch-3 sp, sc in next ch-3 sp, ch 3, shell in shell; ch 1, turn.

Row 16: Sl st in 2 dc and ch-2 sp, beg shell in same sp; shell in next shell; ch 1, turn.

Row 17: Sl st in 2 dc and ch-2 sp, ch 2, dc in shell, Cl in next shell. Finish off; weave in thread ends.

Attach thread to shell of unfinished pineapple; rep Rows 13 to 17. Finish off; weave in thread ends.

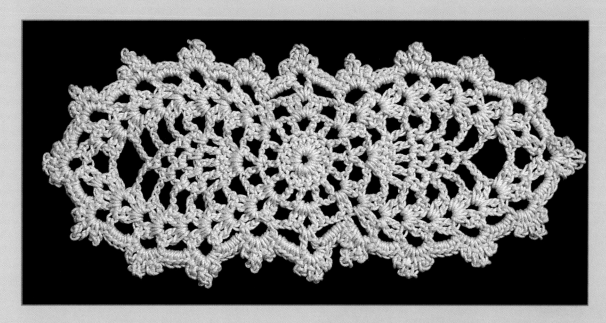

Pineapple Wings

STITCH GUIDE

Beginning Shell (beg shell): In specified st, work (ch 3, dc, ch 2, 2 dc).

Shell (shell): In specified st, work (2 dc, ch 2, 2 dc).

V-Stitch (V-st): In specified st, work (dc, ch 2, dc).

INSTRUCTIONS

Ch 6, join with a sl st to form a ring.

Rnd 1: Ch 3, work 13 dc in ring; join with a sl st in 3rd ch of beg ch-3: 14 dc.

Rnd 2: Ch 5, (counts as a dc and ch-2 sp); *dc in next dc, ch 2; rep from * around; join with a sl st in 3rd ch of beg ch-5.

Rnd 3: Sl st in ch-2 sp, beg shell in same sp; ch 2, skip next sp, V-st in next dc, ch 2; *(skip one ch-2 sp, shell in next ch-2 sp, ch 2) 3 times, skip next sp, V-st in next dc, ch 2, (skip one ch-2 sp, shell in next ch-2 sp, ch 2) twice; join with a sl in 3rd ch of beg ch-3.

Note: *Remainder of pattern is worked in rows.*

Row 1: Sl st in next dc and ch-2 sp, beg shell in same sp; ch 2, 5 dc in V-st, ch 2, shell in shell; ch 1, turn.

Row 2: Sl st in next dc and ch-2 sp, beg shell in same sp; in next 5-dc group work (ch 1, dc in dc) 5 times, ch 1, shell in shell; ch 1, turn.

Row 3: Sl st in dc and ch-2 sp, beg shell in same sp; ch 3, skip one ch-1 sp, (sc in next ch-1 sp, ch 3) 4 times, shell in shell; ch 1, turn.

Row 4: Sl st in dc and ch-2 sp, beg shell in same sp; ch 3, skip one ch-3 sp, (sc in next ch-3 sp, ch 3) 3 times, shell in shell; ch 1, turn.

Row 5: Sl st in dc and ch-2 sp, beg shell in same sp; ch 3, skip one ch-3 sp (sc in next ch-3 sp, ch 3) twice, shell in shell; ch 1, turn.

Row 6: Sl st in dc and ch-2 sp, beg shell in same sp; ch 3, skip one ch-3 sp, sc in next ch-3 sp, ch 3, shell in shell; ch 1, turn work.

Row 7: Sl st in dc and ch-2 sp, beg shell in same sp; ch 2, shell in shell; ch 1, turn.

Row 8: Sl st in dc and ch-2 sp, ch 3, dc in shell, 2 dc in next shell. Finish off; weave in ends.

2nd PINEAPPLE

Skip one shell on Rnd 3, attach thread to next shell, beg shell in same place; complete Rows 1 to 8 once more, do not finish off.

EDGING

Rnd 1: Ch 1, sc in dc; *(ch 3, sc in top of outside st of next of shell)* 8 times, ch 3, V-st in shell, rep *to * 18 times, ch 3, V-st in ch-2 sp of shell; rep from *to* 9 times, ch 3, join with a sl st in first sc.

Rnd 2: Sl st in ch-3 sp, ch 1; *4 sc in ch-3 sp, in next ch-3 sp work (sc, ch 3, sc, ch 5, sc, ch 3, sc); rep from * around, join with a sl st in first sc. Finish off; weave in thread ends.

Pineapples Around

STITCH GUIDE

Beginning Shell (beg shell): In specified st work (ch 3 dc, ch 2, 2 dc).

Shell: In specified st work (2 dc, ch 2, 2 dc).

Beginning Double Shell (beg d-shell): In specified st work [ch 3, dc, (ch 2, 2dc) twice].

Double Shell (d-shell): In specified st work [(2 dc, ch 2) twice, 2 dc].

Puff Stitch (puff st): (YO, insert hook in specified st, YO and draw up a lp) 3 times, YO and draw through all 7 loops on hook, ch 1.

Double Triple Crochet (dtr): YO 3 times; insert hook in specified st and draw up a lp; (YO and draw through 2 lps on hook) 4 times; YO and draw through rem lps on hook.

INSTRUCTIONS

Ch 6, join with a sl st to form a ring.

Rnd 1: (Ch 8, sc in ring) 7 times, ch 3, join with a dtr in first sc.

Rnd 2: Ch 6 (counts as a dc and ch-3 sp), dc in join (top of dtr); *ch 3, in ch-8 sp work, (dc, ch 3, dc); rep from * around; join with a sl st in 3rd ch of beg ch-6.

Rnd 3: Sl st in ch-3 sp, beg shell in same sp; *ch 3, sc in ch-3 sp, ch 3**, shell in next ch-3 sp; rep from * around, end at ** on last rep, join with a sl st in 3rd ch of beg ch-3.

Rnd 4: Sl st in dc and ch-2 sp, beg shell in same sp; *ch 8, shell in shell; rep from * around, ch 8; join with a sl st in 3rd ch of beg ch-3.

Rnd 5: Sl st in dc and ch-2 sp, beg shell in same sp; *ch 3, in ch-8 sp work, (puff st, ch 2) 3 times, puff st, ch 3**, shell in shell; rep from * around, end at ** on last rep, sl st in 3rd ch of beg ch-3.

Rnd 6: Sl st in dc and ch-2 sp, beg shell in same sp; *ch 3, (puff st in ch-2 sp, ch 2) twice, puff st in next ch-2 sp, ch 3**, shell in shell; rep from * around, join with a sl st in 3rd ch of beg ch-3.

Rnd 7: Sl st in dc and ch-2 sp, beg d-shell in same sp; *ch 3, puff st in ch-2 sp, ch 2, puff st in next ch-2 sp, ch 3**, d-shell in shell; rep from * around, end at ** on last rep, join with a sl st in 3rd ch of beg ch-3.

Rnd 8: Sl st in dc and ch-2 sp, beg shell in same sp; *ch 3, shell in next ch-2 sp, ch 3, puff st in next ch-2 sp, ch 3**, shell in ch-2 sp; rep from * around, end at ** on last rep, join with a sl st in 3rd ch of beg ch-3.

Rnd 9: Ch 1, sc in join; *ch 3, skip one st, sc in next st; rep from * around, join with a sl st in first sc. Finish off; weave in ends.

Pineapple Ruffle

STITCH GUIDE

Beginning Shell (beg shell): In specified st work (ch 3, dc, ch 2, 2 dc).

Shell: In specified st, work (2dc, ch 2, 2 dc).

Beginning Double Shell (beg d-shell): In specified st, work [ch 3, dc, (ch 2, 2 dc) twice].

Double Shell (d-shell): In specified st work (2 dc, ch 2) twice.

V-Stitch (V-st): In specified st, work (dc, ch 2, dc).

Picot: Ch 3, sl st in sc at base of ch-3.

INSTRUCTIONS

Ch 6, join with a sl st to form a ring.

Rnd 1: Ch 3, 23 dc in ring; join with a sl st in 3rd ch of beg ch-3: 24 dc.

Rnd 2: Ch 4 (counts as dc and ch-1 sp); *dc in next dc, ch 1; rep from * around; join with a sl st in 3rd ch of beg ch-4.

Rnd 3: Ch 5 (count as dc and ch-2 sp); *dc in next dc, ch 2; rep from * around; join with a sl st in 3rd ch of beg ch-5.

Rnd 4: Sl st in ch-2 sp, ch 6, sl st in 3rd ch of beg ch-6, (dc, picot) twice in same sp; *(dc, picot) twice around the post (vertical bar) of dc, (dc, picot) 3 times in the ch-1 sp of Rnd 2, (dc, picot) twice around the post of next dc**; (dc, picot) 3 times in ch-2 sp; rep from * around, end at ** on last rep, join with a sl st in 3rd ch of beg ch-6. Finish off; weave in ends.

Rnd 5: Attach thread to any free ch-2 sp, beg shell in same sp; *ch 3, V-st in next ch-2 sp, ch 3**, shell in next ch-2 sp; rep from * around; end at ** on last rep, join with a sl st in 3rd ch of beg ch-3.

Rnd 6: Sl st in dc and ch-2 sp, beg shell in same sp; *ch 2, 5 dc in V-st, ch 2**, shell in shell; rep from * around; end at ** on last rep, join with a sl st in 3rd ch of beg ch-3.

Rnd 7: Sl st in dc and ch-2 sp, beg d-shell in same sp; *working on 5-dc group (ch 1, dc in dc) 5 times, ch 1 **, d-shell in shell; rep from * around; end at ** on last rep, join with a sl st in 3rd ch of beg ch-3.

Rnd 8: Sl st in dc and ch-2 sp, beg shell in same sp; *ch 2, shell in next ch-2 sp, ch 3, skip one ch-1 sp; (sc in next ch-1 sp, ch 3) 4 times **; shell in next ch-2 sp; rep from * around, end at **on last rep, join with a sl st in 3rd ch of beg ch-3.

Rnd 9: Sl st in dc and ch-2 sp, beg shell in same sp; *ch 2, dc in ch-2 sp, ch 2, shell in shell, ch 3, skip one ch-3 sp; (sc in next ch-3 sp, ch 3) 3 times **, shell in shell; rep from * around, end at ** on last rep, join with a sl st in 3rd ch of beg ch-3.

Rnd 10: Sl st in dc and ch-2 sp, beg shell in same sp; *ch 3, sc in dc, ch 3, shell in shell, ch 3, skip one ch-3 sp; (sc in next ch-3 sp, ch 3) twice **, shell in shell; rep from * around end at ** on last rep, join with a sl st in 3rd ch of beg ch-3.

Rnd 11: Sl st in dc and ch-2 sp, beg shell in same sp; *(ch 3, dc in ch-3 sp) twice, ch 3, shell in shell, ch 3, skip one ch-3 sp, sc in next ch-3 sp, ch 3**, shell in shell; repeat from * around end at ** on last rep, join with a sl st in 3rd ch of beg ch-3.

Rnd 12: Sl st in dc and ch-2 sp, beg shell in same sp; *(ch 5, sc in ch-3 sp) 3 times, (ch 5, shell in shell**) twice; rep from * around end at ** on last rep, ch 5, join with a sl st in 3rd ch of beg ch-3.

Rnd 13: *Sl st in dc; in ch-2 sp work (sc, picot, sc), sl st in 2 dc; **(6 sc in ch-5 sp) 4 times, sl st in next dc; rep from * to ** once more, in ch-5 sp work, (sc, ch 3) 4 times, sc; repeat from * around, join with a sl st in first sl st. Finish off; weave in ends.

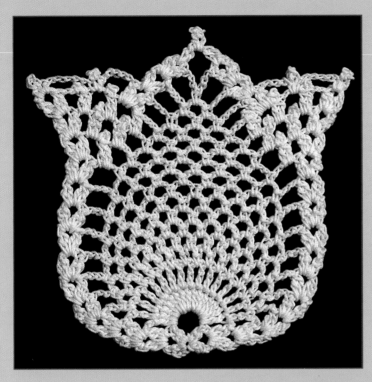

Pineapple Tulip

STITCH GUIDE

Beginning Cluster (beg Cl): In specified st work (ch 2, dc).

Cluster (Cl): (YO, insert hook in specified st, YO and draw up a lp, YO and draw through 2 lps on hook) twice, YO and draw through rem 3 lps on hook.

Beginning Shell (beg shell): In same st work (beg Cl, ch 2, Cl).

Shell: In specified st work (2 Cl, ch 2, 2 Cl).

Picot: Work (ch 3, sl st) in Cl or sc.

INSTRUCTIONS

Row 1: Ch 1; in this ch work (beg Cl, Ch 2, Cl); ch 6; then in same ch at beg of work work (Cl, ch 2, Cl); ch 1, turn.

Row 2: Sl st in ch-2 sp, beg shell in same sp; ch 2, 15 dc in ch-6 sp, ch 2, shell in shell, ch 1, turn.

Row 3: Sl st in ch-2 sp, beg shell in same sp; working in 15 dc group (ch 1, dc in dc) 15 times, ch 1, shell in shell, ch 1, turn.

Row 4: Sl st in ch-2 sp, beg shell in same sp; ch 3, skip one ch-1 sp, (sc in next ch-1 sp, ch 3) 14 times, shell in shell, ch 1, turn.

Row 5: Sl st in ch-2 sp, beg shell in same sp; ch 3, skip one ch-3 sp, (sc in next ch-3 sp, ch 3) 13 times, shell in shell, ch 1, turn.

Row 6: Sl st in ch-2 sp, beg shell in same sp; ch 3, skip one ch-3 sp, (sc in next ch-3 sp, ch 3) 12 times, shell in shell, ch 1, turn.

Row 7: Sl st in ch-2 sp, beg shell in same sp; ch 3, skip one ch-3 sp, (sc in next ch-3 sp, ch 3) 11 times, shell in shell, ch 1, turn.

Row 8: Sl st in ch-2 sp, beg shell in same sp; ch 3, skip one ch-3 sp, (sc in next ch-3 sp, ch 3) 10 times, shell in shell, ch 1, turn.

Row 9: Sl st in ch-2 sp, beg shell in same sp; ch 3, skip one ch-3 sp, (sc in next ch-3 sp, ch 3) 9 times, shell in shell, ch 1, turn.

Row 10: Sl st in ch-2 sp, beg shell in same sp; ch 3, skip one ch-3 sp, (sc in next ch-3 sp, ch 3) 8 times, shell in shell, ch 1, turn.

Row 11: Sl st in ch-2 sp, beg shell in same sp; ch 3, skip one ch-3 sp, (sc in next ch-3 sp, ch 3) 7 times, shell in shell, ch 1, turn.

Row 12: Sl st in ch-2 sp, beg shell in same sp; ch 2, in ch-3 sp work (Cl, picot); ch 3, (sc in next ch-3 sp, ch 3) 6 times; in next ch-3 sp work, (Cl, picot), ch 2, shell in shell; ch 1, turn.

Row 13: Sl st in ch-2 sp, beg shell in same sp; (in next ch-sp work ch 2, Cl, picot) twice, (ch 3, sc in next ch-3 sp) 5 times; ch 3, (in next ch-sp work Cl, picot, ch 2) twice, shell in shell; ch 1, turn.

Row 14: Sl st in ch-2 sp, beg shell in same sp; (in next ch-sp work ch 2, Cl, picot) 3 times, (ch 3, sc in next ch-3 sp) 4 times; ch 3, (in next ch-sp work Cl, picot, ch 2) 3 times, shell in shell; ch 1, turn.

Row 15: Sl st in ch-2 sp, ch 1, (sc, picot, sc) in shell; ch 5, skip one ch-2 sp, (sc, picot, sc) in next ch-2 sp, ch 5, shell in next ch-2 sp, ch 3, skip one ch-3 sp, (sc in next ch-3 sp, ch 3) 3 times, skip one ch-3 sp, shell in next ch-2 sp, ch 5, (sc, picot, sc) in next ch-2 sp, ch 5, (sc, picot, sc) in shell. Finish off; weave in ends. Turn.

Row 16: Attach yarn to last shell made, beg shell; ch 3, skip one ch-3 sp, (sc in next ch-3 sp, ch 3) twice, shell in shell, ch 1, turn.

Row 17: Sl st in ch-2 sp, beg shell in same sp; ch 3, skip one ch-3 sp, sc in next ch-3 sp, ch 3, shell in shell, ch 1, turn.

Row 18: Sl st in ch-2 sp, beg Cl in same sp; Cl in next shell, ch 1, turn, sl st between Cl, sc, picot, sc. Finish off; weave in thread ends.

Puff Stitch Pineapple

STITCH GUIDE

Beginning Puff Stitch (beg puff st): Ch 2, (YO, insert hook in specified st, YO and draw up a lp) twice, YO and draw through all 5 lps on hook; ch 1.

Puff Stitch (puff st): (YO, insert hook in specified st, YO and draw up a lp) 3 times, YO and draw through all 7 loops on hook; ch 1.

Beginning Shell (beg shell): In specified st work (beg puff st, ch 2, puff st).

Shell: In specified st work (puff st, ch 2, puff st).

Beginning Double Shell (beg d-shell): In specified st work beg puff st, (ch 2, puff st) twice.

Double Shell (d-shell): In specified st work (puff st, ch 2) twice, puff st in same st.

V- Stitch (V-st): In specified st work (dc, ch 3, dc).

Picot: Ch 3 sl st in first ch.

INSTRUCTIONS

Ch 6, join with a sl st to form a ring.

Rnd 1: Ch 6 (counts as dc and ch-3 sp); (dc in ring, ch 3) 5 times, sl st in 3rd ch of beg ch-6.

Rnd 2: Ch 6 (counts as dc and ch-3 sp), dc in join (first V-st made); *ch 3, V-st in next dc; rep from * around, ending with 6th V-st, join with a dc in 3rd ch of beg ch-6.

Rnd 3: Sl st in ch-3 sp, beg shell in same sp; *ch 2, in V-st work, (sc, ch 3) 4 times, sc, ch 2**, shell in next ch-3 sp; rep from * around, end at ** on last rep; join with a sl st in beg puff st.

Rnd 4: Sl st in ch-2 sp, beg shell in same sp; *ch 3, (sc in next ch-3 sp, ch 3) 4 times**, shell in shell; rep from * around, end at ** on last rep; join with a sl st in beg puff st.

Rnd 5: Sl st in ch-2 sp, beg d-shell in same sp; *ch 3, skip one ch-3 sp, (sc in next ch-3 sp, ch 3) 3 times**, d-shell in shell; rep from * around, end at ** on last rep; join with a sl st in beg puff st.

Rnd 6: Work beg shell; *ch 3, shell in next ch-2 sp, ch 3, skip one ch-3 sp, (sc in next ch-3 sp, ch 3) twice**, shell in ch-2 sp; rep from * around, end at ** on last rep; join with a sl st in beg puff st.

Rnd 7: Sl st in ch-2 sp, beg shell in same sp; *(ch 3, shell in ch-3 sp) twice, ch 3, skip one ch-3 sp, sc in next ch-3 sp, ch 3**, shell in shell; rep from * around, end at ** on last rep;join with a sl st in beg puff st.

Rnd 8: Sl st in ch-2 sp, beg shell in same sp; *(ch 3, sc in ch-3 sp, ch 3, shell in shell) twice, ch 2**, shell in shell; rep from * around, end at ** on last rep; join with a sl st in beg puff st.

Rnd 9: Sl st in ch-2 sp, ch 1; *[(sc, picot, sc) in shell, ch 8] twice, (sc, picot, sc) in next two ch sps; rep from* around, join with a sl st in first sc. Finish off; weave in ends.

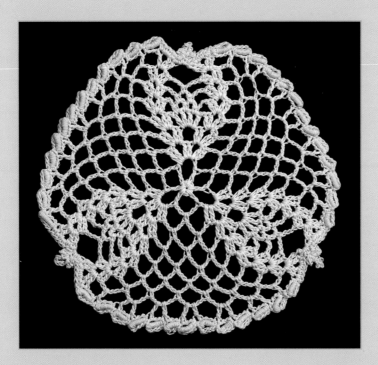

Pineapple Triplets

STITCH GUIDE

Beginning Shell (beg shell): In specified st work (ch 3, dc, ch 2, 2 dc).

Shell: In specified st work (2 dc, ch 2, 2 dc).

Beginning Double Shell (beg d-shell): In specified st work [ch 3, dc, (ch 2, 2 dc) twice].

Double Shell (d-shell): In specified st work [(2 dc, ch 2) twice, 2 dc].

Bullion St: Wrap thread 12 times around hook, insert hook in specified st, YO and draw through all lps on hook, ch 1.

Picot Cluster (picot-Cl): In last sc made work (ch 3, sl st, ch 5, sl st, ch 3, sl st).

V-Stitch (V-st): In specified st work (dc, ch 3, dc).

INSTRUCTIONS

Ch 6, join with a sl st to form a ring.

Rnd 1: Ch 8 (counts as dc and ch-5 sp); *(dc in ring, ch 5) 4 times, dc in ring, ch 1, join with a tr in 3rd ch of beg ch-8.

Rnd 2: Beg d-shell; *ch 5, sc in next ch-5 sp, ch 5**, d-shell in next ch-5 sp; rep from *around, end at ** on last rep; join with a sl st in 3rd ch of beg ch-3.

Rnd 3: Sl st in dc and ch-2 sp, beg shell in same sp; *ch 3, shell in next ch-2 sp, (ch 5, sc in next ch-5 sp) twice, ch 5**, shell in next ch-2 sp; rep from * around, end at ** on last rep; join with a sl st in 3rd ch of beg ch-3.

Rnd 4: Sl st in dc and ch-2 sp, beg shell in same sp; *in ch-3 sp work (ch 1, dc) 4 times, ch 1, shell in shell, (ch 5, sc in ch-5 sp) 3 times, ch 5**, shell in shell; rep from * around, end at ** on last rep, sl st in 3rd ch of beg ch-3.

Rnd 5: Sl st in dc and ch-2 sp, beg shell in same sp; *ch 3, skip one ch-1 sp, (sc in next ch-1 sp, ch 3) 3 times, shell in shell, (ch 5, sc in next ch-5 sp) 4 times, ch 5**, shell in shell; rep from * around, end at ** on last rep, sl st in 3rd ch of beg ch-3.

Rnd 6: Sl st in dc and ch-2 sp, beg shell in same sp;* ch 3, skip one ch-3 sp, (sc in next ch-3 sp, ch 3) twice, shell in shell, (ch 5, sc in next ch-5 sp) 5 times, ch 5**, shell in shell; rep from * around, end at ** on last rep; sl st in 3rd ch of beg ch-3.

Rnd 7: Sl st in dc and ch-2 sp, beg shell in same sp; *ch 3, skip one ch-3 sp, sc in next ch-3 sp, ch 3, shell in shell, (ch 5, sc in ch-5 sp) 6 times, ch 5**, shell in shell; rep from * around, end at ** on last rep, join with a sl st in 3rd ch of beg ch-3.

Rnd 8: Sl st in dc and ch-2 sp, beg shell in same sp, ch 1, * shell in next shell, ch 3, dc in ch-5 sp, (ch 3, V-st in next ch-5 sp) 5 times, ch 3, dc in next ch-5 sp, ch 3 ** shell in next shell, ch 1; rep from * around, end at ** on last rep, join with a sl st in 3rd ch of beg ch-3.

Rnd 9: Ch 1; *sc in next 6 sts, in next ch sp work, (sc, picot-Cl, sc), sc in next 6 sts, (bullion st in next dc, ch 3, sl st in same dc) 13 times; rep from * around, join with a sl st in first sc. Finish off; weave in ends.

Pineapple Angel Wings

STITCH GUIDE

Beginning Shell (beg shell): In specified st work (ch 3, dc, ch 3, 2 dc).

Shell: In specified st work (2 dc, ch 3, 2 dc).

Double Shell (d-shell): In specified st work [(2 dc, ch 3) twice, 2 dc].

Popcorn Stitch (PC): In specified st work 4 dc; drop lp from hook, insert hook in top of first dc, insert hook in dropped loop and draw lp through.

Picot: Work (ch 3, sl st) in PC.

INSTRUCTIONS

Ch 6, join with a sl st to form a ring.

Rnd 1: Ch 1, 12 sc in ring, join with a sl st in first sc.

Rnd 2: Ch 1, sc in join; *ch 3, skip one sc, sc in next sc; rep from * around; ch 3, join with a sl st in first sc: 6 ch-3 lps.

Rnd 3: Sl st in ch-3 sp, beg shell in same sp; (shell in next ch-3 sp) twice, ch 5, (shell in next ch-3 sp) 3 times, ch 5; join with a sl st in 3rd ch of beg ch-3.

Rnd 4: Sl st in dc and ch-3 sp, beg shell in same sp; (shell in next shell) twice, ch 3, in ch-5 sp work (3 dc, ch 4, 3 dc), ch 3, (shell in shell) 3 times, ch 3, in ch-5 sp work, (3 dc, ch 4, 3 dc), ch 3; join with a sl st in 3rd ch of beg ch-3.

Rnd 5: Sl st in dc and ch-3 sp, beg shell in same sp; (shell in shell) twice, ch 2, *skip 2 dc and ch 3, (dc in next st, ch 1) 9 times, dc in next st, ch 2**, (shell in shell) 3 times; rep from * to ** once more; join with a sl st in 3rd ch of beg ch-3.

Rnd 6: Sl st in dc and ch-3 sp, beg shell in same sp; (shell in shell) twice; *ch 3, PC in ch-1 sp, ch 1, dc in next 7 sts, ch 1, in next ch-1 sp work (PC, ch 3, PC), dc in next 7 sts, ch 1, PC in next ch-1 sp, ch 3**; (shell in shell) 3 times, rep from * to ** once more; join with a sl st in 3rd ch of beg ch-3.

Rnd 7: Sl st in dc and ch-3 sp, beg shell in same sp; (shell in shell) twice; ch 5, *PC in ch-1 sp, ch 1, skip 1dc, dc in next 5 dc, ch 1, PC in next sp**, ch 3, shell in next ch-3 sp, ch 3 rep from * to ** once more, ch 5***, (shell in shell) 3 times, ch 5; rep from * to *** once more; join with a sl st to 3rd ch of beg ch-3.

Rnd 8: Sl st in dc and ch-3 sp, beg shell in same sp; (shell in shell) twice; *ch 5, sc in ch-5 sp, ch 5, **(PC in ch-1 sp, ch 1, skip 1 dc, dc in next 3 dc, ch 1, PC in next ch-1 sp)***, ch 3, d-shell in shell, ch 3, rep from ** to *** once more, ch 5, sc in ch-5 sp, ch 5 ****, (shell in shell) 3 times; rep from * to **** once more; join with a sl st in 3rd ch of beg ch-3.

Rnd 9: Sl st in dc and ch-3 sp, beg shell in same sp; (shell in shell) twice; *ch 5 (sc in ch 5 sp, ch 5) twice, **(PC in ch-1 sp, ch 1, skip 1 dc, dc in next dc, ch 1, PC in next ch-1 sp)***, (ch 3, shell in ch-3) twice, ch 3, rep from ** to *** once more, ch 5, (sc in ch-5 sp, ch 5) twice ****, (shell in shell) 3 times; rep from * to **** once more; join with a sl st in 3rd ch of beg ch-3.

Rnd 10: Sl st in dc and next 2 ch sts, ch 1, sc in shell, (ch 5, sc in next ch sp) 5 times; *ch 5, PC in ch-1 sp, ch 1, PC in next ch-1 sp, (ch 5, sc in ch-3 sp) 5 times, ch 5, PC in ch-1 st, ch 1, PC in next ch-1 sp** (ch 5, sc in next ch-sp) 9 times; rep from * to ** once more, (ch 5, sc in next sp) 3 times, ch 5; join with a sl st in first sc.

Rnd 11: Ch 1 sc in join; (ch 5, sc in sc) 5 times, ch 5, PC in ch-1 sp, picot, (ch 5, sc in sc) 5 times, ch 5, PC in ch-1 sp, picot, (ch 5, sc in sc) 9 times, ch 5, PC in ch-1 sp, picot, (ch 5, sc in sc) 5 times, ch 5, PC in ch-1 sp, picot, (ch 5, sc in sc) 3 times, ch 5; join with a sl st in first sc. Finish off; weave in ends.

Pineapple Squared

STITCH GUIDE

V-Stitch (V-st): In specified st work (dc, ch 3, dc).

INSTRUCTIONS

Ch 49.

Row 1: Dc in 5th ch from hook and in each rem ch; ch 3, turn.

Row 2: Skip first dc, dc in next 3 dc; *(ch 2, skip 2 dc, dc in next dc) 5 times; ch 2, skip 2 dc, dc in next 4 dc, (ch 2, skip 2 dc, dc in next dc) 6 times; dc in last 3 dc.

Row 3: Dc in next 3 dc; *(ch 2, dc in next dc) 5 times; 2 dc in ch-2 sp, dc in next dc, ch 2, skip 2 dc, dc in next dc, 2 dc in ch-2 sp, (dc in next dc, ch 2) 5 times; dc in next 4 dc, ch 3, turn.

Row 4: Dc in 3 dc; *(ch 2, dc in next dc) 4 times; 2 dc in ch-2 sp, dc in dc, ch 2, V-st in next ch-2 sp; ch 2, skip 3 dc, dc in next dc, 2 dc in ch-2 sp; (dc in next dc, ch 2) 4 times, dc in next 4 dc, ch 3, turn.

Row 5: Dc in 3 dc; *(ch 2, dc in next dc) 3 times, 2 dc in ch-2 sp, dc in next dc, ch 3, 7 dc in V-st; ch 3, skip 3 dc, dc in next dc, 2 dc in ch-2 sp; (dc in next dc, ch 2) 3 times, dc in next 4 dc, ch 3, turn.

Row 6: Dc in 3 dc; *(ch 2, dc in next dc) twice, 2 dc in ch-2 sp, dc in next dc, ch 3, skip 3 dc, working in 7 dc group (dc in next dc, ch 1) 6 times; dc in next dc, ch 3, skip 3 dc, dc in next dc, 2 dc in ch-2 sp, (dc in next dc, ch 2) twice; dc in next 4 dc, ch 3, turn .

Row 7: Dc in 3 dc, ch 2, dc in next dc, 2 dc in ch-2 sp, dc in next dc, ch 5; (sc in ch-1 sp, ch 3) 5 times, sc in next ch-1 sp, ch 5, skip 3 dc, dc in next dc; 2 dc in ch-2 sp, dc in next dc, ch 2, dc in 4 dc, ch 3, turn.

Row 8: Dc in 3 dc, 2 dc in ch-2 sp, dc in next dc, ch-8, (sc in ch-3 sp, ch 3) 4 times; sc in next ch-3 sp, ch 8, skip 3 dc, dc in next dc, 2 dc in ch-2 sp, dc in next 4 dc, ch 3, turn.

Row 9: Dc in 3 dc, ch 2, skip 2 dc, dc in next dc, 3 dc in ch-8 sp, ch 5, (sc in ch-3 sp, ch 3) 3 times; sc in next ch-3 sp, ch 5, 3 dc in ch-8 sp, dc in next dc, ch 2, skip 2 dc, dc in 4 dc, ch 3, turn.

Row 10: Dc in 3 dc,;ch 2, dc in next dc, ch 2, skip 2 dc, dc in next dc, 3 dc in ch-5 sp; ch 5, (sc in ch-3 sp, ch 3) twice, sc in next ch-3 sp, ch 5, 3 dc in ch-5 sp; dc in next dc, ch 2, skip 2 dc, dc in next dc, ch 2, dc in 4 dc, ch 3, turn.

Row 11: Dc in 3 dc; *(ch 2, dc in next dc) twice, ch 2, skip 2 dc, dc in next dc, 3 dc in ch-5 sp, ch 5, sc in ch-3 sp, ch 3, sc in next ch-3 sp, ch 5; 3 dc in ch-5 sp, dc in dc, ch 2, skip 2 dc, (dc in next dc, ch 2) twice, dc in 4 dc, ch 3, turn.

Row 12: Dc in 3 dc; *(ch 2, dc in next dc) 3 times, ch 2, skip 2 dc, dc in next dc, 3 dc in ch-5 sp, ch 5; sc in ch-3 sp, ch 5, 3 dc in ch-5 sp, dc in dc, ch 2, skip 2 dc, (dc in next dc, ch 2) 3 times, dc in 4 dc, ch 3, turn.

Row 13: Dc in 3 dc; *(ch 2, dc in next dc) 4 times, ch 2, skip 2 dc, dc in next dc, 3 dc in ch-5 sp; ch 2, 3 dc in next ch-5 sp, dc in dc, ch 2, skip 2 dc, (dc in next dc, ch 2) 4 times, dc in next 4 dc, ch 3, turn.

Row 14: Dc in 3 dc; *(ch 2, dc in next dc) 5 times, ch 2, skip 2 dc, dc in next dc, 2 dc in next ch-2 sp, dc in next dc, ch 2, skip 2 dc, (dc in next dc, ch 2) 5 times, dc in 4 dc, ch 3, turn.

Row 15: Dc in next 3 dc (2 dc in 2-ch sp, dc in next dc) 6 times, dc in next 3 dc, (2 dc in 2-ch sp, dc in next dc) 6 times, dc in last 3 dc. Finish off; weave in ends.

Pineapple Hexagon

STITCH GUIDE

Beginning Shell (beg shell): In specified st work (ch 3, dc, ch 2, 2 dc).

Shell: In specified st work (2 dc, ch 2, 2 dc).

Beginning Double Shell (beg d-shell): In specified st work ([ch 3, dc (ch 2, 2 dc) twice].

Double Shell (d-shell): In specified st work [(2 dc, ch 2) twice, 2 dc].

Popcorn Stitch (PC): In specified st work 4 dc; drop lp from hook, insert hook from front to back in top of first dc, pick up dropped lp and draw through lp on hook.

V-Stitch (V-st): In specified st work (dc, ch 2, dc).

Picot: Ch 3, sl st in first ch made.

INSTRUCTIONS

Ch 6; join with a sl st to form a ring.

Rnd 1: Ch 1, 12 sc in ring; join with a sl st in first sc.

Rnd 2: Ch 5 (counts as dc and ch-2 sp); *dc in next sc, ch 2; rep from * around; join with a sl st in 3rd ch of beg ch-5.

Rnd 3: Ch 5 (counts as dc and ch-2 sp), dc in join; *2 dc in ch-2 sp, V-st in dc; rep from * around; 2 dc in ch-2 sp; join with a sl st in 3rd of beg ch-5.

Rnd 4: Sl st in ch-2 sp, beg shell in same sp; *ch 2, V-st in V-st, ch 2**, shell in next V-st; rep from * around, end at ** on last rep; join with a sl st in 3rd ch of beg ch-3.

Rnd 5: Sl st in dc and ch-2 sp, beg shell in same sp; *ch 2, 4 dc in V-st, ch 2**, shell in shell; rep from * around, end at ** on last rep; join with a sl st in 3rd ch of beg ch-3.

Rnd 6: Sl st in dc and ch-2 sp, beg d-shell in same sp; *ch 2 in 4-dc group (dc in next dc, ch-1) 3 times, dc in next dc, ch 2**, d-shell in shell; rep from * around, end at ** on last rep; join with a sl st in 3rd ch of beg ch-3.

Rnd 7: Sl st in dc and ch-2 sp, beg shell in same sp; *ch 2, shell in next ch-2 sp, ch 3, (PC in ch-1 sp, ch 2) twice, PC in next ch-1 sp, ch 3**, shell in next ch-2 sp; rep from * around, end at ** on last rep; join with a sl st in 3rd ch of beg ch-3.

Rnd 8: Sl st in dc and ch-2 sp, beg shell in same sp; *ch 3, PC in next ch-2 sp, ch 3, shell in shell, ch 3, PC in ch-2 sp between PC, ch 2, PC in next ch-2 sp, ch 3**, shell in shell; rep from * around, end at ** on last rep; join with a sl st in 3rd ch of beg ch-3.

Rnd 9: Sl st in dc and ch-2 sp, beg shell in same sp; *ch 3, PC in ch-3 sp, ch 2, PC in next ch-3 sp, ch 3, shell in shell, ch 3, PC in next ch-2 sp between PC, ch 3**, shell in shell; rep from * around, end at ** on last rep; join with a sl st in 3rd ch of beg ch-3.

Rnd 10: Sl st in dc and ch-2 sps, ch 1; *sc in shell, ch 7, PC in ch-2 sp between PC, ch 7, sc in shell, (ch 5, sc in ch-3 sp) twice, ch 5; rep from * around, join with a sl st in first sc.

Rnd 11: Sl st in ch-7 sp, ch 1; *9 sc in ch-7 sp, picot, 9 sc in next ch-7 sp, (5 sc in ch-5 sp) 3 times; rep from * around, join with a sl st in first sc. Finish off; weave in ends.

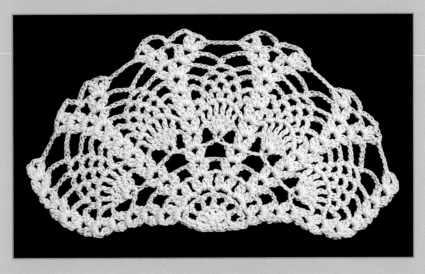

Pineapple Fan

STITCH GUIDE

Beginning Cluster (beg Cl): In specified st work (ch 2, dc).

Cluster (Cl): *YO, insert hook in specified st, YO and draw up a lp, YO and draw through 2 lps on hook; rep from * once in same st, YO and draw through rem 3 lps on hook.

Beginning Shell (beg shell): Work (beg cl, ch 2, cl) in specified st.

Shell: Work (2 cl, ch 2, 2 cl) in specified st.

Double Shell (d-shell): Work [(2 cl, ch 2) twice, 2 cl] in specified st.

INSTRUCTIONS

Ch 4.

Row 1: Work 6 dc in first ch, ch 5, turn.

Row 2: Skip first dc (dc in next dc, ch 2) 5 times; dc in 3rd ch of turning ch, ch 1, turn.

Row 3: (Sc in dc, ch 3) 6 times; sc in 3rd ch of turning ch. Ch 1; do not turn work.

Row 4: Rotate piece to work straight edge of semi-circle as follows: sl st in turning ch, ch 1, now working over turning ch or post (vertical bar) of end dc, work 2 sc over end of each of next 2 rows, sc in ch-1 st at center, work 2 sc over end of each of next 2 rows, sl st in sc. Cl 1; do not turn work.

Row 5: Rotate piece to work rounded edge again. Sl st in ch-3 sp, beg shell in same sp; (ch 2, shell in ch-3 sp) 5 times, ch 1, turn.

Row 6: Sl st in ch-2 sp, beg shell in same sp; (ch 3, shell in shell) 5 times, ch 1, turn.

Row 7: Sl st in ch-2 sp, beg shell in same sp; *ch 7, sl st in 6th ch from hook: ring formed, ch 2, shell in shell; rep from * across, ch 1 turn.

Row 8: Sl st in ch-2 sp, beg shell in same sp; *ch 1, 6 dc in ch-5 ring, ch 1, shell in shell; rep from * across, ch 1 turn.

Row 9: Sl st in ch-2 sp, beg shell in same sp; *(ch 1, dc in next dc of 6 dc group) 6 times, ch 1, shell in shell; rep from * across, ch 1, turn.

Row 10: Sl st in ch-2 sp, beg shell in same sp; *ch 3, skip one ch-1 sp, (sc in next ch-1 sp, ch 3) 5 times, shell in shell; rep from * across, ch 1, turn.

Row 11: Sl st in ch-2 sp, beg shell in same sp; *ch 3, skip one ch-3 sp, (sc in next ch-3 sp, ch 3) 4 times, shell in shell; rep from * across, ch 1, turn.

Row 12: Sl st in ch-2 sp, beg shell in same sp; *ch 3, skip one ch-3 sp, (sc in next ch-3 sp, ch 3) 3 times, shell in shell; rep from * across, ch 1, turn.

Row 13: Sl st in ch-2 sp, beg shell in same sp; *ch 3, skip one ch-3 sp, (sc in next ch-3 sp, ch 3) twice**, d-shell in shell; rep from * across, end at ** on last rep, shell in shell, ch 1, turn.

Row 14: Sl st in ch-2 sp, beg shell in same sp; *ch 5, skip one ch-3 sp, sc in next ch-3 sp, ch 5**, shell in ch-2 sp, ch 3, shell in next ch-2 sp; rep from * across, end at ** on last rep, shell in shell, ch 1, turn.

Row 15: Sl st in ch-2 sp, beg shell in same sp; *ch 5, shell in shell**, ch 5, sc in ch-3 sp, ch 5, shell in shell; rep from * across, end at ** on last rep. Finish off; weave in ends.

Pineapple Petals

STITCH GUIDE

Beginning Shell (beg shell): In specified st work (ch 3, dc, ch 2, 2 dc).

Shell: In specified st work (2 dc, ch 2, 2 dc).

V-Stitch (V-st): In specified st work (dc, ch 2, dc).

Picot: Ch 3, sl st in first ch.

INSTRUCTIONS

Center

Ch 6; join with a sl st to form a ring.

Rnd 1 (right side): Ch 1, 12 sc in ring; join with a sl st in first sc.

Rnd 2: Ch 3, dc in join; *2 dc in next sc; rep from * around; join with a sl st in 3rd of ch-3: 24 dc.

Rnd 3: Ch 1, sc in join; *ch 5, skip 2 dc, sc in next dc; rep from * around; ch 5, join with a sl st in first sc: 8 ch-5 sps.

Rnd 4: Working behind Rnd 3, sc in next dc on Rnd 2; *ch 5, sc in first of next 2 skipped dc on Rnd 2; rep from * around; ch 5, join with sc in first sc: 8 ch-5 sps.

Rnd 5: Working behind Rnd 4, *ch 5, sc in next skipped dc on Rnd 2; rep from * around; ch 2, join with a sl st in first sc: 8 ch-5 sps; finish off.

Note: *You now have 3 rnds of 8 ch-5 sps each; remainder of pattern is worked in rows, with each overlapping pineapple worked separately.*

First Pineapple Petal

Row 1: With right side facing, join thread with a sl st in any ch-5 sp of Center Rnd 5; work beg shell in same sp; ch 2, V-st in next ch-5 sp on Center Rnd 4; ch 3, shell in next ch-5 sp on Center Rnd 3; ch 1, turn.

Row 2: Sl st in 2 dc and ch-2 sp, beg shell in same sp; ch 2, 6 dc in V-st, ch 2, shell in shell, ch 1, turn.

Row 3: Sl st in 2 dc and ch-2 sp, beg shell in same sp; working in 6-dc group (ch 1, dc in dc) 6 times, ch 1, shell in shell, ch 1, turn.

Row 4: Sl st in 2 dc and ch-2 sp, beg shell in same sp; ch 3, skip one ch-1 sp, (sc in next ch-1 sp, ch 3) 5 times, shell in shell, ch 1 turn.

Row 5: Sl st in 2 dc and ch-2 sp, beg shell in same sp; ch 3, skip one ch-3 sp, (sc in next ch-3 sp, ch 3) 4 times, shell in shell, ch 1, turn.

Row 6: Sl st in 2 dc and ch-2 sp, beg shell in same sp; ch 3, skip one ch-3 sp, (sc in next ch-3 sp, ch 3) 3 times, shell in shell, ch 1, turn.

Row 7: Sl st in 2 dc and ch-2 sp, beg shell in same sp; ch 3, skip one ch-3 sp, (sc in next ch-3 sp, ch 3) twice, shell in shell, ch 1, turn.

Row 8: Sl st in 2 dc and ch-2 sp, beg shell in same sp; ch 3, skip one ch-3 sp, sc in next ch-3 sp, ch 3, shell in shell, ch 1, turn.

Row 9: Sl st in 2 dc and ch-2 sp, beg shell in same sp; ch 2, shell in shell, ch 1, turn.

Row 10: Sl st in 2 dc and ch-2 sp, (ch 3, dc) in same sp; 2 dc in next shell, picot, turn; join with a sl st in 3rd ch of beg ch-3. Finish off; weave in ends.

Second Pineapple Petal

Join thread in next unused ch-5 sp on Center Rnd 5. Work Rows 1 through 10 of First Pineapple Petal.

Third through Eighth Pineapple Petals

Work as for Second Pineapple Petal.

Pineapple Star Points

STITCH GUIDE

Beginning Shell (beg shell): In specified sp work (ch 3, dc, ch 2, 2 dc).

Shell: In specified st work (2 dc, ch 2, 2 dc).

Beginning Double Shell (beg d-shell): In specified st work [ch 3, dc, (ch 2, 2 dc) twice].

Double Shell (d-shell): In specified st work [(2 dc, ch 2) twice, 2 dc].

V-Stitch (V-st): In specified st work (tr, ch 3, tr).

Picot: Ch 3, sl st in dc/sc.

Double Triple Crochet (dtr): YO 3 times, insert hook in specified st, YO and draw up a lp; (YO and draw through 2 lps on hook) 4 times.

Picot Cluster (picot-Cl): In specified st work (ch 3, sl st, dtr, ch 5; sl st in same place as last sl st, ch 3, sl st in same place as last sl st).

Love Knot: Draw up a lp 1/2" high, YO and draw through lp, sc in back lp of st.

INSTRUCTIONS

Ch 6; join with a sl st to form a ring.

Rnd 1: Ch 3 (counts as first dc), in ring work dc, (ch 3, 2 dc) 4 times; ch 3, join with a sl st in 3rd ch of beg ch-3.

Rnd 2: Ch 3, dc in join, 2 dc in next dc; *ch 2, sc in ch-3 sp, ch 2**, (2 dc in next dc) twice; rep from * around, end at ** on last rep; join with a sl st in 3rd ch of beg ch-3.

Rnd 3: Ch 3, dc in next dc; *ch 3, dc in next 2 dc; repeat from * around; ch 3, join with a sl st in 3rd ch of beg ch-3.

Rnd 4: Sl st in dc and ch-3 sp, beg d-shell in same sp; *ch 2, 4 dc in ch-3 sp, ch 2**; d-shell in next ch-3 sp; rep from * around, end at ** on last rep; join with a sl st in 3rd ch of beg ch-3.

Rnd 5: Sl st in dc and ch-2 sp, beg shell in same sp; *ch 2, shell in next ch-2 sp, (ch 1, dc in next dc of 4-dc group) 4 times, ch 1**; shell in next ch-2 sp; rep from * around, end at ** on last rep; join with a sl st in 3rd ch of beg ch-3.

Rnd 6: Sl st in dc and ch-2 sp, beg shell; *ch 4, shell in next shell, love knot, skip one ch-1 sp; (sc in next ch-1 sp, ch 3) twice, sc in next ch-1 sp, love knot**, shell in shell; rep from * around, end at ** on last rep, join with a sl st in 3rd ch of beg ch-3.

Rnd 7: Sl st in dc and ch-2 sp, beg shell; * in ch-4 sp work (love knot, V-st, love knot), shell in shell, love knot; sc in ch-3 sp, ch 3, sc in next ch-3 sp, love knot**, shell in next shell; rep from * around, end at ** on last rep; join with a sl st in 3rd ch of beg ch-3.

Rnd 8: Sl st in dc and ch-2 sp; in ch-2 sp work, (ch 3, dc, picot, 2 dc); *3 love knots, dtr in V-st, picot-Cl, 3 love knots; in next shell work (2 dc, picot, 2 dc), love knot; in ch-3 sp work (sc, picot, sc), love knot**; in next shell work, (2 dc, picot, 2 dc); rep from * around; end at ** on last rep, join with a sl st in 3rd ch of beg ch-3. Finish off; weave in thread ends.

Pineapple Square

STITCH GUIDE

Beginning Shell (beg shell): In specified st work (ch 3, dc, ch 2, 2 dc).

Shell: In specified st work (2 dc, ch 2, 2 dc).

Beginning Double Shell (beg d-shell): In specified st work [ch 3, dc, (ch 2, 2 dc) twice].

Double Shell (d-shell): In specified st work [(2 dc, ch 2) twice, 2 dc].

Cluster (Cl): (YO, insert hook in specified st, YO and draw up a lp, YO and draw through 2 lps on hook) twice, YO and draw through rem 3 lps on hook.

Picot: Ch 3, sl st in sc at base of ch-3.

V-Stitch (V-st): In specified st work (dc, ch 2, dc).

Large V-Stitch (large V-st): In specified st work (dc, ch 3, dc).

INSTRUCTIONS

Ch 6; join with a sl st to form a ring.

Rnd 1: Ch 1, 16 sc in ring; join with a sl st in first sc.

Rnd 2: Ch 1, sc in join; *ch 3, skip one sc, sc in next sc; rep from * around, ch 1; join with a hdc in first sc.

Rnd 3: Ch 1, sc in join; *ch 4, sc in next ch-3 sp; rep from * around, ch 2; join with a hdc in first sc.

Rnd 4: Ch 1, sc in join; ch 5, sc in next ch-4 sp; rep from * around, ch 1, tr in first sc.

Rnd 5: Beg d-shell; *ch 5, sc in next ch-5 sp, ch 5**, d-shell in next ch-5 sp; rep from * around, end at ** on last rep; join with a sl st in 3rd ch of beg ch-3.

Rnd 6: Sl st in dc and ch-2 sp, beg shell in same sp; *ch 3, shell in next ch-2 sp, ch 3, sc in next ch-5 sp, ch 5, sc in next ch-5 sp, ch 3**, shell in next ch-2 sp; rep from * around, end at ** on last rep; join with a sl st in 3rd ch of beg ch-3.

Rnd 7: Sl st in dc and ch-2 sp, beg shell in same sp; *ch 2, V-st in ch-3 sp, ch 2, shell in shell, ch 3, 5 dc in ch-5 sp, ch 3**, shell in shell; rep from * around, end at ** on last rep; join with a sl st in 3rd ch of beg ch-3 .

Rnd 8: Sl st in dc and ch-2 sp, beg shell in same sp; *(ch 3, dc in V-st) 3 times, ch 3, shell in shell, ch 2, (dc in next dc of 5-dc group, ch 1) 4 times, dc in next dc, ch 2**, shell in shell; rep from * around, end at ** on last rep; join with a sl st in 3rd ch of beg ch-3.

Rnd 9: Sl st in dc and ch-2 sp, beg shell in same sp; *ch 3, skip one ch-3 sp, (large V-st in next ch-3 sp, ch 3) twice; shell in shell, (ch 3, sc in ch-1 sp) 4 times; ch 3**, shell in shell; rep from * around, end at ** on last rep; join with a sl st in 3rd ch of beg ch-3.

Rnd 10: Sl st in dc and ch-2 sp, beg shell in same sp; *skip one ch-3 sp, (in next ch-3 sp work (ch 3, dc) 3 times, ch 3, dc in next ch-3 sp; (in next ch-3 sp work (ch 3, dc) 3 times, ch 3, shell in shell, ch 3, skip one ch-3 sp, (sc in next ch-3 sp, ch 3) 3 times**, shell in shell; rep from * around, end at ** on last rep; join with a sl st in 3rd ch of beg ch-3.

Rnd 11: Sl st in dc and ch-2 sp, beg shell in same sp; *ch 3, skip one ch-3 sp, (dc in next ch-3 sp, ch 3) twice, (in next ch-3 sp work large V-st, ch 3) twice; (dc in next ch-3 sp, ch 3) twice, shell in shell, ch 3, skip one ch-3 sp, (sc in next ch-3 sp, ch 3) twice**, shell in shell; rep from * around, end at ** on last rep; join with a sl st in 3rd ch of beg ch-3.

Rnd 12: Sl st in next 3 sts, ch 1; *sc in next 2 dc, 3 sc in next ch-3 sp, (in next ch-3 sp work, 2 sc, picot, 2 sc) 7 times, 3 sc in next ch-3 sp, sc in 2 dc, ch 3, (Cl, picot) in shell, skip one ch-3 sp, (Cl, picot) in next ch-3 sp, Cl, in next shell, ch 3; rep from * around, join with a sl st in first sc. Finish off; weave in ends.

Pineapple Whirlygig

STITCH GUIDE

Beginning Shell (beg shell): In specified st work (ch 3, dc, ch 2, 2 dc).

Shell: In specified st work (2 dc, ch 2, 2 dc).

Beginning Double Shell (beg d-shell): In specified st work [ch 3, dc, (ch 2, 2 dc) twice].

Double Shell (d-shell): In specified st work [(2 dc, ch 2) twice, 2 dc].

Beginning V-Stitch (beg V-st): Ch 6, dc in same place as join.

V-Stitch (V-st): In specified st work (dc, ch 3, dc).

Puff stitch (puff st): (YO, insert hook in specified st, YO and draw up a lp) 4 times, YO and draw through all loops on hook; ch 1.

Picot: Ch 5, sl st in puff st.

INSTRUCTIONS

Ch 6; join with a sl st in to form a ring.

Rnd 1: Ch 1, 12 sc in ring; join with a sl st in first sc.

Rnd 2: Ch 1, sc in join; *ch 3, skip one sc, sc in next sc; rep from * around, ch 1, join with hdc in first sc.

Rnd 3: Work beg V-st; *ch 3, V-st in next ch-3 sp; rep from * around, ch 3, join with a sl st in 3rd ch of beg ch-6.

Rnd 4: Sl st in ch-3 sp, beg shell in same sp; *ch 3, sc in next ch-3 sp, ch 3**, shell in V-st; rep from * around, end at ** on last rep; join with a sl st in 3rd ch of beg ch-3.

Rnd 5: Sl st in dc and ch-2 sp, beg shell in same sp; *(ch 3, sc in ch-3 sp) twice, ch 3**, shell in next shell; rep from * around, end at ** on last rep; join with a sl st in 3rd ch of beg ch-3.

Rnd 6: Sl st in dc and ch-2 sp, beg d-shell in same sp; *ch 2, skip one ch-3 sp, 5 dc in next ch-3 sp, ch 2**, d-shell in next shell; rep from * around, end at ** on last rep; join with a sl st in 3rd ch of beg ch-3.

Rnd 7: Sl st in dc and ch-2 sp, beg shell in same sp; *ch 3, shell in next ch-2 sp, (ch 1, dc in next dc of 5-dc group) 5 times, ch 1**, shell in next ch-2 sp; rep from * around, end at ** on last rep; join with a sl st in 3rd ch of beg ch-3.

Rnd 8: Sl st in dc and ch-2 sp, beg shell in same sp; *ch 3, sc in ch-3 sp, ch 3, shell in next shell, ch 3, skip one ch-1 sp; (sc in next ch-1 sp, ch 3) 4 times**, shell in next shell; rep from * around, end at ** on last rep; join with a sl st in 3rd ch of beg ch-3.

Rnd 9: Sl st in dc and ch-2 sp, beg shell in same sp; *(ch 3, sc in next ch-3 sp) twice, ch 3, shell in next shell, ch 2, skip one ch-3 sp; (puff st in next ch-3 sp, ch 2) 3 times**, shell in next shell; rep from * around, end at ** on last rep; join with a sl st in 3rd ch of beg ch-3.

Rnd 10: Sl st in dc and ch-2 sp, beg shell in same sp; *(ch 3, sc in next ch-3 sp) 3 times, ch 3, shell in next shell, ch 2, skip one ch-2 sp; (puff st in next ch-2 sp, ch 2) twice **, shell in next shell; rep from * around, end at ** on last rep; join with a sl st in 3rd ch of beg ch-3.

Rnd 11: Sl st in dc and ch-2 sp, beg shell in same sp; *(ch 3, sc in next ch-3 sp) 4 times, ch 3, shell in next shell, ch 2, skip one ch-2 sp; puff st in next ch-2 sp, ch 2 **, shell in next shell; rep from * around, end at ** on last rep; join with a sl st in 3rd ch of beg ch-3.

Rnd 12: Sl st in dc and ch-2 sp, beg shell in same sp; *ch 3, sc in next ch-3 sp, ch 10, skip three ch-3 sps, sc in next ch-3 sp, ch 3, shell in next shell, ch 3**, shell in next shell; rep from * around, end at ** on last rep; join with a sl st in 3rd ch of beg ch-3.

Rnd 13: Ch 1, sc in join, sc in next 9 sts; *in ch-10 sp work (puff st, picot) 7 times, puff st; skip next sc**, sc in next 22 sts; rep from * around, end at ** on last rep; join with a sl st in first sc. Finish off; weave in ends.

Pointed Pineapple

STITCH GUIDE

Beginning Cluster (beg Cl): In specified st work (ch 2, dc).

Cluster (Cl): *(YO, insert hook in specified st, YO and draw up a lp, YO and draw through 2 lps on hook) twice, YO and draw through rem 3 lps on hook.

Beginning Shell (beg shell): In specified st work (beg Cl, ch 2, Cl).

Shell: In specified st work (Cl, ch 2, Cl).

Beginning Double Shell (beg d-shell): In specified st work [beg Cl, (ch 2, Cl) twice].

Double Shell (d-shell): In specified st work [(Cl, ch 2) twice, Cl].

V-Stitch (V-st): In specified st work (dc, ch 2, dc).

Picot Cluster (picot-Cl): In last sc made work (ch 3, sl st in 3rd ch from hook, ch 5, sl st in 5th ch from hook, ch 3, sl st in 3rd ch from hook.)

INSTRUCTIONS

Ch 6; join with a sl st to form a ring.

Rnd 1: Ch 1, 12 sc in ring; join with a sl st in first sc.

Rnd 2: Beg Cl in same sc; *ch 2, Cl in next sc; rep from * around, ch 2, sl st in beg Cl.

Rnd 3: Sl st in ch-2 sp, beg shell in same sp, *ch 3, skip one ch-2 sp, shell in next ch-2; rep from * around, ch 3, join with a sl st in beg Cl.

Rnd 4: Sl st in ch-2 sp, beg d-shell in same sp; *ch 3, d-shell in shell; rep from * around, ch 3, join with a sl st in beg Cl.

Rnd 5: Sl st in ch-2 sp, beg shell in same sp; *ch 3, shell in next ch-2 sp, ch 3, shell in next ch-2 sp; rep from * around, ch 3, join with a sl st in beg Cl.

Rnd 6: Sl st in ch-2 sp, beg shell in same sp; *ch 3, sc in ch-3 sp, ch 3, shell in shell, ch 2, V-st in ch-3 sp, ch 2**, shell in shell; rep from * around, end at ** on last rep, join with a sl st in beg Cl.

Rnd 7: Sl st in ch-2 sp, beg shell in same sp; *(ch 3, sc in ch-3 sp) twice, ch 3, shell in shell, ch 2, 5 dc in V-st, ch 2**, shell in shell; rep from * around, end at ** on last rep, join with a sl st in beg Cl.

Rnd 8: Sl st in ch-2 sp, beg d-shell in same sp; *ch 2, skip one ch-3 sp, V-st in ch-3 sp, ch 2, d-shell in shell, (ch 1, dc in next dc of 5 dc group) 5 times, ch 1**, d-shell in shell; rep from * around, end at ** on last rep, join with a sl st in beg Cl.

Rnd 9: Sl st in ch-2 sp, beg shell in same sp; *shell in next ch-2 sp, ch 2, 3 dc in V-st, ch 2, (shell in next ch-2 sp) twice, ch 3, skip one ch-1 sp, (sc in next ch-1 sp, ch 3) 4 times**, shell in ch-2 sp; rep from * around, end at ** on last rep, join with a sl st in beg Cl.

Rnd 10: Sl st in ch-2 sp, beg shell in same sp; *ch 2, shell in shell, (ch 1, dc in dc) 3 times, ch 1, shell in shell, ch 2, shell in shell, ch 3, skip one ch-3 sp, (sc in next ch-3 sp, ch 3) 3 times**, shell in shell; rep from * around, end at ** on last rep, join with a sl st in beg Cl.

Rnd 11: Sl st in ch-2 sp, beg shell in same sp; *ch 3, shell in shell, ch 3, skip one ch-1 sp, (sc in next ch-1 sp, ch 3) twice, (shell in shell, ch 3) twice, skip one ch-3 sp, (sc in next ch-3 sp, ch 3) twice**, shell in shell; rep from * around, end at ** on last rep, join with a sl st in beg Cl.

Rnd 12: Sl st in ch-2 sp, beg shell; *ch 3, in next ch-3 sp work (sc, picot-Cl, sc), ch 3, shell in shell, ch 3, skip one ch-3 sp, sc in next ch-3 sp, ch 3, shell in shell, ch 3 in next ch-3 sp work (sc, picot-Cl, sc), ch 3, shell in shell, ch 3, skip one ch-3 sp, sc in next ch-3 sp, ch 3, shell in shell; rep from * around, join with a sl st in beg Cl. Finish off; weave in ends.

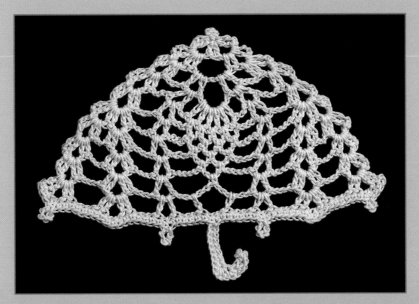

Pineapple Parasol

STITCH GUIDE

Beginning Shell (beg shell): In specified st work (ch 3, dc, ch 3, 2 dc).

Shell (shell): In specified st work (2 dc, ch 3, 2 dc).

Beginning Double Shell (beg d-shell): In specified st work [ch 3, dc, (ch 3, 2 dc) twice].

Double shell (d-shell): In specified st work [(2 dc, ch 3) twice, 2 dc].

V-Stitch (V-st): In specified st work (dc, ch 2, dc).

Picot: Ch 5, sl st in sc at base of ch-5.

INSTRUCTIONS

Ch 5; join with a sl st to form a ring.

Row 1: Work beg d-shell in join; ch 1, turn.

Row 2: Sl st in dc and ch-3 sp, beg shell in same sp; ch 6, shell in next ch-3 sp; ch 1, turn.

Row 3: Sl st in dc and ch-3 sp, beg shell in same sp; ch 3, in ch-6 sp work (V-st, ch 6, V-st); ch 3, shell in shell; ch 1, turn.

Row 4: Sl st in dc and ch-3 sp, beg shell in same sp; ch 3, V-st in V-st, ch 2, in ch-6 sp work (dc, ch 1) 5 times; dc in same ch-6 sp, ch 2; V-st in V-st, ch 3, shell in shell; ch 1, turn.

Row 5: Sl st in dc and ch-3 sp, beg shell in same sp; ch 3, V-st in V-st, (ch 3, sc in ch-1 sp) 5 times, ch 3, V-st in V-st, ch 3, shell in shell; ch 1, turn.

Row 6: Sl st in dc and ch-3 sp, beg d-shell in same sp; ch 3, V-st in V-st, ch 4, skip one ch-3 sp, (sc in next ch-3 sp, ch 3) 3 times, sc in next ch-3 sp, ch 4, V-st in V-st, ch 3, d-shell in shell; ch 1, turn.

Row 7: Sl st in dc and ch-3 sp, beg shell in same sp; ch 2, shell in next ch-3 sp, ch 3, V-st in V-st, ch 4, (sc in ch-3 sp, ch 3) twice, sc in next ch-3 sp, ch 4, V-st in V-st, ch 3, shell in ch-3 sp, ch 2, shell in next ch-3 sp; ch 1, turn.

Row 8: Sl st in dc and ch-3 sp, beg shell in same sp; ch 3, shell in shell, ch 3, V-st in V-st, ch 5, sc in ch-3 sp, ch 3, sc in next ch-3 sp, ch 5, V-st in V-st, (ch 3, shell in shell) twice; ch 1, turn.

Row 9: Sl st in dc and ch-3 sp, beg shell in same sp; ch 3, shell in shell, ch 3, V-st in V-st, ch 6, sc in ch-3 sp, ch 6, V-st in V-st, (ch 3, shell in shell) twice; ch 1, turn.

Row 10: Sl st in dc and ch-3 sp, beg shell in same sp; ch 3, shell in shell, ch 3, V-st in V-st, (ch 3, dc in ch-6 sp) twice, ch 3, V-st in V-st, (ch 3, shell in shell) twice; ch 1, turn.

Row 11: Sc in next 4 sts, picot, sc in each st to center of V-st, picot, sc in each st to center of row to work handles: ch 17, (sc dec in next 2 sts) 3 times, 4 sc dec, sc in next 7 ch sts, sl st in last sc worked on parasol edge before handle, continuing along edge, sc in each st to center of next V-st, picot, sc in each st to center of last shell, picot, sc in last 4 sts. Finish off; weave in ends.

Pineapple Star

STITCH GUIDE

Beginning Shell (beg shell): In specified st work (ch 3, dc, ch 2, 2 dc).

Shell: In specified st work (2 dc, ch 2, 2 dc).

Cluster (Cl): (YO, insert hook in specified st, YO and draw up a lp, YO and draw through 2 loops on hook) twice, YO and draw through rem loops on hook.

Picot: Ch 3, sl st in sc at base of ch-3.

INSTRUCTIONS

Ch 6; join with a sl st to form a ring.

Rnd 1: Ch 1, 12 sc in ring; join with a sl st in first sc.

Rnd 2: Ch 1, sc in join; *ch 3, skip one sc, sc in next sc; rep from * around, ch 3; join with a sl st in first sc.

Rnd 3: Sl st in ch-3 sp; *in ch-3 sp work, (sc, hdc, 3 dc, hdc, sc): petal made; rep from * around, join with a sl st in first sc.

Rnd 4: Working behind petals, ch 1; sc in back strand of first sc on first petal; *ch 4, sc in back strand of first sc on next petal, ch 4; rep from * around, join with a sl st in first sc.

Rnd 5: Sl st in ch-4 sp; *in ch-4 sp work (sc, hdc, 5 dc, hdc, sc): petal made; rep from * around, join with a sl st in first sc.

Rnd 6: Working behind petals, ch 1, sc in back strand of first sc on first petal, ch 5; *sc in back strand of first sc on next petal, ch 5; rep from * around; join with a sl st in first sc.

Rnd 7: Sl st in ch-4 sp; *in ch-5 sp work, (sc, hdc, 7 dc, hdc, sc), rep from * around, join with a sl st in first sc.

Rnd 8: Working behind petals, ch 1, sc in back strand of first sc on first petal, ch 6; *sc in back strand of first sc on next petal, ch 6; rep from * around, sl st in first sc.

Rnd 9: Sl st in ch-6 sp; *in ch-6 sp work, (sc, hdc, 9 dc, hdc, sc); rep from * around, join with a sl st in first sc.

Rnd 10: Working behind petals, ch 1, sc in back strand of first sc on first petal, ch 7; *sc in back strand of first sc on next petal, ch 7; rep from * around, sl st in first sc.

Rnd 11: Sl st in ch-7 sp, work beg shell in same sp; ch 2, shell in same sp; *in next ch-7 sp work (shell, ch 2, shell; rep from * around, join with a sl st in 3rd ch of beg ch-3.

Rnd 12: Sl st in dc and ch-2 sp, work beg shell in same sp; *ch 2, 5 dc in next ch-2 sp, ch 2, shell in next shell) **; shell in next shell; rep from * around, end at ** on last rep, join with a sl st in 3rd ch of beg ch-3.

Rnd 13: Sl st in dc and ch-2 sp, beg shell in same sp; *(ch 1, dc in next dc of 5-dc group) 5 times, ch 1, shell in next shell ** shell in next shell; rep from * around, end at **; on last repeat, join with a sl st in 3rd ch of ch-3.

Rnd 14: Sl st in dc and ch-2 sp, beg shell in same sp; *ch 3, skip one ch-1 sp, (sc in next ch-1 sp, ch 3) 4 times, shell in next shell**; shell in next shell; rep from * around, end at ** on last rep, join with a sl st in 3rd ch of ch-3.

Note: *Remainder of pattern is worked in rows.*

Row 1: Sl st in dc and ch-2 sp, beg shell in same sp; ch 3, skip one ch-3 sp, (sc in next ch-3 sp, ch 3) 3 times, shell in shell, ch 1, turn.

Row 2: Sl st in dc and ch-2 sp, beg shell in same sp; ch 3, skip one ch-3 sp, (sc in next ch-3 sp, ch 3) twice, shell in shell, ch 1, turn work.

Row 3: Sl st in dc and ch-2 sp, beg shell in same sp; ch 3, skip one ch-3 sp, sc in next ch-3 sp, ch 3, shell in shell, ch 1, turn.

Row 4: Sl st in dc and ch-2 sp, beg shell in same sp; ch 2, shell in shell, ch 1, turn.

Row 5: Sl st in dc and ch-2 sp, ch 2, dc in front shell, Cl in next shell; ch 1, turn; work (sc, picot, sc) between Cl. Finish off; weave in ends.

To complete unfinished pineapples work as follows: attach thread to next unfinished pineapple, rep Rows 1 to 5.

Pineapple Christmas

STITCH GUIDE

Beginning Shell (beg shell): In specified st work (ch 3, dc, ch 2, 2 dc, ch 2, dc).

Shell: In specified st work [dc, (ch 2, 2 dc) twice].

INSTRUCTIONS

Ch 33.

Row 1 (right side): Dc in 5th ch from hook and in each rem ch across, ch 1, turn.

Row 2: Sl st in first dc, sl st and work beg shell in next dc; (ch 2, skip 2 dc, dc in next dc) 8 times; ch 2, skip 2 dc, shell in next dc, leave ch-4 turning ch unworked; ch 1, turn.

Row 3: Sl st in next 6 sts and ch-2 sp, work beg shell in same sp; skip dc and ch-2 sp, (dc in next dc, ch 2) 3 times, skip one ch-2 sp, 5 dc in next ch-2 sp; ch 2, skip next dc, dc in next dc, (ch 2, dc in next dc) twice, skip one ch-2 sp, shell in next ch-2 sp; ch 1, turn.

Row 4: Sl st in next 6 sts and ch-2 sp, beg shell; skip next 2 dc and ch-2 sp, (dc in next dc, ch 2) twice, (dc in next dc, ch 1) 4 times, (dc in next dc, ch 2) twice; dc in next dc, skip one ch-2 sp, shell in next ch-2 sp; ch 1, turn.

Row 5: Sl st in next 6 sts and ch-2 sp, beg shell; skip next 2 dc and ch-2 sp, dc in next dc, ch 5, (sc in next ch-1 sp, ch 3) 3 times; sc in next ch-1 sp, ch 5, skip dc and ch-2 sp, dc in next dc; skip next ch-2 sp, shell in next ch-2 sp; ch 1, turn.

Row 6: Sl st in next 6 sts and ch-2 sp, beg shell; dc in ch-5 sp, ch 5, (sc in ch-3 sp, ch 3) twice; sc in next ch-3 sp, ch 5, dc in ch-5 sp, shell in ch-2 sp; ch 1, turn.

Row 7: Sl st in next 6 sts and ch-2 sp, beg shell; dc in ch-5 sp, ch 5, sc in ch-3 sp, ch 3, sc in next ch-3 sp, ch 5; dc in ch-5 sp, shell in ch-2 sp; ch 1, turn.

Row 8: Sl st in next 6 sts and ch-2 sp, beg shell; dc in ch-5 sp, ch 5, sc in ch-3 sp, ch 5; dc in ch-5 sp, shell in ch-2 sp; ch 1, turn.

Row 9: Sl st in next 6 sts and ch-2 sp, beg shell; dc in ch-5 sp, ch 2, dc in next ch-5 sp, shell in ch-2 sp; ch 1, turn.

Row 10: Sl st in next 6 sts and ch-2 sp, beg shell; skip one ch-2 sp, shell in next ch-2 sp; ch 1, turn.

Row 11: Sl st in next 6 sts and ch-2 sp, ch 3, dc in same ch-2 sp, ch 1, 2 dc in next ch-2 sp; ch 1, turn.

Row 12: Sl st in 2 dc; ch 6, (sl st in ch-1 sp, ch 5) 5 times; sl st in first sl st; finish off.

Row 13 (tree trunk): Hold piece with right side facing and Row 12 at the bottom. Join thread to base of 14th dc on Row 1; ch 3 (counts as a dc), dc in next 3 dc, ch 3, turn.

Row 14: Dc in next 3 dc, ch 1, turn.

Row 15: Sc in next 4 dc. Finish off; weave in thread ends.

Pineapple Popcorns

STITCH GUIDE

Beginning Popcorn Stitch (beg PC): In specified st work (ch-3, 3 dc); drop lp from hook, insert hook from front to back in 3rd ch of beg ch-3, pick up dropped lp and draw through lp on hook.

Popcorn Stitch (PC): In specified st work 4 dc; drop lp from hook, insert hook from front to back in top of first dc, pick up dropped lp and draw through lp on hook.

Beginning Shell (beg shell): In specified st work (beg PC, ch 3, PC).

Shell (shell): In specified st work (PC, ch 3, PC).

Beginning Double Shell (beg d-shell): In specified st work [beg PC, (ch 3, PC) twice].

Double Shell (d-shell): In specified st work [(PC, ch 3) twice, PC].

Picot: Ch 3, sl st in first ch made.

V-Stitch (V-st): In specified st work (dc, ch 3, dc).

INSTRUCTIONS

Ch 8; join with a sl st to form a ring.

Rnd 1: Sl st in ring, work beg PC in ring; *(ch 3, PC in ring) 7 times; ch 3, join with a sl st in beg PC.

Rnd 2: Sl st in ch-3 sp, beg shell in same sp; *ch 2, V-st in next ch-3 sp, ch 2**, shell in next ch-3 sp; rep from * around, end at ** on last rep; join with a sl st in beg PC.

Rnd 3: Sl st in ch-3 sp, beg shell in same sp; *ch 2, 8 dc in V-st, ch 2**, shell in next shell; rep from * around, end at ** on last rep; join with a sl st in beg PC.

Rnd 4: Sl st in ch-3 sp, beg shell in same sp; *(ch 1, dc in next dc of 8-dc group) 8 times, ch 1**, shell in next shell; rep from * around, end at ** on last rep; join with a sl st in beg PC.

Rnd 5: Sl st in ch-3 sp, beg shell in same sp; *ch 3, skip one ch-1 sp, (sc in next ch-1 sp, ch 3) 7 times**, shell in next shell; rep from * around, end at ** on last rep; join with a sl st in beg PC.

Rnd 6: Sl st in ch-3 sp, beg d-shell in same sp; *ch 3, skip one ch-3 sp, (sc in next ch-3 sp, ch-3) 6 times**, d-shell in next shell; rep from * around, end at ** on last rep; join with a sl st in beg PC.

Rnd 7: Sl st in ch-3 sp, beg shell in same sp; *ch 5, shell in next ch-3 sp, ch 5, skip one ch-3 sp, (sc in next ch-3 sp, ch 3) 4 times, sc in next ch-3 sp, ch 5**, shell in next ch-3 sp; rep from * around, end at ** on last rep; join with a sl st in beg PC.

Rnd 8: Sl st in ch-3 sp, beg shell in same sp; *ch 3, d-shell in ch-5 sp, ch 3, shell in next shell, ch 5, (sc in ch-3 sp, ch 3) 3 times, sc in next ch-3 sp, ch 5**, shell in next shell; rep from * around, end at ** on last rep; join with a sl st in beg PC.

Rnd 9: Sl st in ch-3 sp, beg shell in same sp; *ch 3, skip one ch-3 sp, shell in next ch-3 sp, ch 5, shell in next ch-3 sp, ch 5, skip one ch-3 sp, shell in next shell, ch 5, (sc in next ch-3 sp, ch-3) twice, sc in next ch-3 sp, ch 5**, shell in next shell; rep from * around, end at ** on last rep; join with a sl st in beg PC.

Rnd 10: Sl st in ch-3 sp, beg shell in same sp; *ch 5, shell in next shell, ch 3, d-shell in ch-5 sp, ch 3, shell in next shell, ch 5, shell in next shell, ch 5, sc in next ch-3 sp, ch 3, sc in next ch-3 sp, ch 5**, shell in next shell; rep from * around, end at ** on last rep; join with a sl st in beg PC.

Rnd 11: Sl st in ch-3 sp, beg shell in same sp; *ch 5, shell in next shell, skip one ch-3 sp, (ch 5, shell in next ch-3 sp) twice, (ch 5, shell in next shell) twice, ch 5, sc in ch-3 sp, ch 5**, shell in next shell; rep from * around, end at ** on last rep; join with a sl st in beg PC.

Rnd 12: Sl st in ch-3 sp, beg shell in same sp; *(ch 5, shell in next shell) twice, in next ch-5 sp work (ch 5, shell) twice, (ch 5, shell in next shell) 3 times**, ch 2, shell in next shell; rep from * around, end at ** on last rep; join with hdc in beg PC.

Rnd 13: Work (ch 1, sc, picot, sc) in same sp as join; *(ch 4, sl st in 3rd ch from hook, ch 2, sc in next sp) 16 times**; work (picot, sc) in same sp; rep from * around, end at ** on last rep join with a sl st in first sc. Finish off; weave in ends.

Perfect Pineapple

STITCH GUIDE

Beginning Shell (beg shell): In specified st work (ch 3, 2 dc, ch 3, 3 dc).

Shell (shell): In specified st work (3 dc, ch 3, 3 dc).

Beginning Double Shell (beg d-shell): In specified st work [ch 3, 2 dc, (ch 3, 3 dc) twice].

Double Shell (d-shell): In specified st work [(3 dc, ch 3) twice, 3 dc].

Picot: Ch 3, sl st in dc.

INSTRUCTIONS

Ch 8; join with a sl st to form a ring.

Rnd 1: Ch 1, 16 sc in ring, join with a sl st in first sc.

Rnd 2: Ch 3, dc in next 3 sc; *ch 5, dc in next 4 sc; rep from * around, ch 1, join with a tr in 3rd ch of beg ch-3.

Rnd 3: Work beg shell; *ch 6, sl st in 5th ch from hook, ch 2**, shell in next ch-5 sp; rep from * around, end at ** on last rep; join with a sl st in 3rd ch of beg ch-3.

Rnd 4: Sl st in 2 dc and ch-3 sp, beg shell in same sp; *ch 3, 5 dc in ch-5 picot, ch 3**, shell in shell; rep from * around, end at ** on last rep; join with a sl st in 3rd ch of beg ch-3.

Rnd 5: Sl st in 2 dc and ch-3 sp, beg d-shell in same sp; *ch 2, (dc in next dc of 5-dc group, ch 1) 4 times, dc in next dc, ch 2**, d-shell in shell; rep from * around, end at ** on last rep; join with a sl st in 3rd ch of beg ch-3.

Rnd 6: Sl st in 2 dc and ch-3 sp, beg shell in same sp; *ch 5, shell in next ch-3 sp, ch 5, (sc in ch-1 sp, ch 3) 3 times, sc in next ch-1 sp, ch 5**, shell in next ch-3 sp; rep from * around, end at ** on last rep; join with a sl st in 3rd ch of beg ch-3.

Rnd 7: Sl st in 2 dc and ch-3 sp, beg shell in same sp; *ch 3, in ch 5 sp work, (dc, picot) 3 times, dc, ch 3, shell in shell, ch 5, (sc in ch-3 sp, ch 3) twice, sc in next ch-3 sp, ch 5**, shell in shell; rep from * around, end at ** on last rep; join with a sl st in 3rd ch of beg ch-3.

Rnd 8: Sl st in 2 dc and ch-3 sp, beg shell in same sp, *ch 3, (dc in next dc of dc-picot group, ch 3, sl st in first ch, ch 1) 3 times, dc in next dc, ch 3, shell in shell, ch 5, sc in ch-3 sp, ch 3, sc in next ch-3 sp, ch 5**, shell in shell; rep from * around, end at ** on last rep; join with a sl st in 3rd ch of beg ch-3.

Rnd 9: Sl st in 2 dc and ch-3 sp, beg shell; *ch 3, (dc in next dc of dc-picot grou, ch 4, sl st in 2nd ch, ch 2) 3 times, dc in next dc, ch 3, shell in shell, ch 5, sc in ch-3 sp, ch 5**, shell in shell; rep from * around, end at ** on last rep; join with a sl st in 3rd of ch-3.

Rnd 10: Sl st in 2 dc and ch-3 sp, beg shell in same sp; *(ch 5, sl st in 3rd ch, ch 3, dc in next dc) 4 times; ch 5, sl st in 3rd ch, ch 3, shell in shell, ch 4, sl st in 2nd ch, ch 2**; shell in shell; rep from * around, end at ** on last rep; join with a sl st in 3rd ch of beg ch-3. Finish off; weave in ends.

Pineapple Filigree

STITCH GUIDE

Beginning Shell (beg shell): In specified st work (ch 3, dc, ch 3, 2 dc).

Shell (shell): In specified st work (2 dc, ch 3, 2 dc).

Beginning double Shell (beg d-shell): In specified st work [ch 3, dc, (ch 2, 2 dc) twice].

Double shell (d-shell): In specified st work [(2 dc, ch 2) twice, 2 dc].

V-Stitch (V-st): In specified st work (dc, ch 3, dc).

Picot: Ch 3, sl st in first ch made.

INSTRUCTIONS

Ch 6; join with a sl st to form a ring.

Rnd 1: Ch 1, 12 sc in ring; join with a sl st in first sc.

Rnd 2: Ch 3, dc in next sc; *ch 8, skip one sc, dc in next 2 sc; rep from * around, ch 8, sl st in 3rd ch of beg ch-3.

Rnd 3: Ch 3, dc in join; *ch 2, 2 dc in next dc, ch 3, sc in ch-8 sp, ch 3**, 2 dc in next dc; rep from * around, end at ** on last rep; join with a sl st in 3rd ch of beg ch-3.

Rnd 4: Sl st in dc and ch-2 sp, beg shell in same sp; *ch 3, V-st in sc, ch 3**, shell in shell; rep from * around, end at ** on last rep; join with a sl st in 3rd ch of beg ch-3.

Rnd 5: Sl st in dc and ch-2 sp, beg d-shell in same sp; *ch 3, 6 dc in V-st, ch 3**, d-shell in shell; rep from * around, end at ** on last rep; join with a sl st in 3rd ch of beg ch-3.

Rnd 6: Sl st in dc and ch-2 sp, beg shell in same sp; *ch 3, shell in next ch-2 sp, ch 2, (dc in next dc of 6-dc group, ch 1) 5 times, dc in next dc, ch 2**, shell in ch-2 sp; rep from * around, end at ** on last rep; join with a sl st in 3rd ch of beg ch-3.

Rnd 7: Sl st in dc and ch-2 sp, beg shell in same sp; *ch 3, dc in ch-3 sp, ch 3, shell in shell, (ch 3, sc in ch-1 sp) 5 times, ch 3**, shell in shell; rep from * around, end at ** on last rep; join with a sl st in 3rd ch of beg ch-3.

Rnd 8: Sl st in dc and ch-2 sp, beg shell in same sp; *(ch 3, dc in ch-3 sp) twice, ch 3, shell in shell, ch 3, skip one ch-3 sp, (sc in next ch-3 sp, ch 3) 4 times**, shell in shell; rep from * around, end at ** on last rep; join with a sl st in 3rd ch of beg ch-3.

Rnd 9: Sl st in dc and ch-2 sp, beg shell in same sp; *ch 3, dc in ch-3 sp, ch 3, V-st in next ch-3 sp, ch 3, dc in next ch-3 sp, ch 3, shell in shell, ch 3, skip one ch-3 sp, (sc in next ch-3 sp, ch 3) 3 times**, shell in shell; rep from * around, end at ** on last rep; join with a sl st in 3rd ch of bg ch-3.

Rnd 10: Sl st in dc and ch-2 sp, beg shell in same sp; *(ch 3, dc in next ch-3 sp) twice, ch 3, V-st in V-st, (ch 3, dc in next ch-3 sp) twice, ch 3, shell in shell, ch 3, skip one ch-3 sp, (sc in next ch-3 sp, ch 3) twice**, shell in shell; rep from * around, end at ** on last rep; join with a sl st in 3rd ch of beg ch-3.

Rnd 11: Sl st in dc and ch-2 sp, beg shell in same sp; *(ch 3, dc in ch-3 sp) 3 times, ch 3, V-st in V-st, (ch 3, dc in next ch-3 sp) 3 times, ch 3, shell in shell, ch 3, skip one ch-3 sp, sc in next ch-3 sp, ch 3**, shell in shell; rep from * around, end at ** on last rep; join with a sl st in 3rd ch of beg ch-3.

Rnd 12: Sl st in dc and ch-2 sp, beg shell; *(ch 3, dc in next ch-3 sp) 4 times, ch 3, in V-st work (dc, ch 6, dc); (ch 3, dc in next ch-3 sp) 4 times, ch 3, (shell in shell) **, twice; rep from * around, end at ** on last rep, join with a sl st in 3rd ch of ch-3.

Rnd 13: Ch 1, sc in next 6 sts; *in each next five ch-3 sps work, (sc, hdc, 2 dc, hdc, sc); in next ch-5 sp work, (sc, hdc, 3 dc, picot, 2 dc, hdc, sc); in next five ch-3 sps work, (sc, hdc, 2 dc, hdc, sc)**, sc in next 12 sts; rep from * around, end at ** on last rep; sc in next 6 sts, join with a sl st in first sc. Finish off; weave in ends.

Pineapple Parade

STITCH GUIDE

Beginning Shell (beg shell): In specified st work (ch 3, dc, ch 3, 2 dc).

Shell: In specified st work (2 dc, ch 3, 2 dc).

Beginning Double Shell (beg d-shell): In specified st work [ch 3, dc, (ch 3, 2 dc) twice].

Double Shell (d-shell): In specified st work [(2 dc, ch 3) twice, 2 dc].

Picot: Ch 3, sl st in sc/dc.

INSTRUCTIONS

Ch 6; join with a sl st to form a ring.

Rnd 1: Ch 8 (counts as a dc and ch-5); *(dc in ring, ch 5) 5 times, dc in ring, ch 1; join with a tr in 3rd ch of ch-8: 7 ch-5 lps made.

Rnd 2: Beg shell; *ch 5, shell in next ch-5 sp; rep from * around, ch 5; join with a sl st in 3rd ch of beg ch-3.

Rnd 3: Sl st in dc and ch-3 sp, beg shell in same sp; *in ch-5 sp work, (sc, hdc, 2 dc, ch 1, 2 dc, hdc, sc)**, shell in shell; rep from * around, end at ** on last rep; join with a sl st in 3rd ch of beg ch-3.

Rnd 4: Sl st in dc and ch-3 sp, beg shell in same sp; *ch 2, 5 dc in ch-1 sp, ch 2**, shell in shell; rep from * around, end at ** on last rep; join with a sl st in 3rd ch of beg ch-3.

Rnd 5: Sl st in dc and ch-3 sp, beg d-shell in same sp; *(ch 1, dc in next dc of 5-dc group) 5 times, ch 1**, d-shell in shell; rep from * around, end at ** on last rep; join with a sl st in 3rd ch of beg ch-3.

Rnd 6: Sl st in dc and ch-3 sp, beg shell in same sp; *shell in next ch-3 sp, ch 3, skip one ch-1 sp, (sc in next ch-1 sp, ch 3) 4 times**; skip one ch-3 sp, shell in next ch-3 sp; rep from * around, end at ** on last rep; join with a sl st in 3rd ch of beg ch-3.

Rnd 7: Sl st in dc and ch-3 sp, beg shell in same sp; *ch 5, shell in shell, ch 3, skip one ch-3 sp; (sc in next ch-3 sp, ch 3) 3 times**, shell in shell; rep from * around, end at ** on last rep; join with a sl st in 3rd ch of beg ch-3.

Rnd 8: Sl st in dc and ch-3 sp, beg shell in same sp; *ch 5, sc in ch-5 sp, ch 5, shell in shell, ch 3, skip one ch-3 sp, (sc in next ch-3 sp, ch 3) twice**; shell in shell; rep from * around, end at ** on last rep; join with a sl st in 3rd ch of beg ch-3.

Rnd 9: Sl st in dc and ch-3 sp, beg shell in same sp; * ch 5, (sc in next ch-5 sp, ch 5) twice, shell in shell, ch 3, skip one ch-3 sp, sc in next ch-3 sp, ch 3**, shell in shell; rep from * around, end at ** on last rep; join with a sl st in 3rd ch of beg ch-3.

Rnd 10: Sl st in dc and ch-3 sp, beg shell in same sp; *ch 5, sc in ch-5 sp, 10 dc in next ch-5 sp, sc in next ch-5 sp, ch 5, shell in shell** shell in shell; rep from * around, end at ** on last rep; join with a sl st in 3rd ch of beg ch-3.

Rnd 11: Sl st in dc and next two ch sts, ch 1, sc; *ch-5, (dc in next dc of 10-dc group, ch 1) 9 times, dc in next dc, ch-5, sc in shell**, ch 3, sc in shell; rep from * around, end at ** on last rep; join with a dc in first sc.

Rnd 12: Ch 3, dc, (picot, 2 dc) twice in same sp as join; *5 sc in ch-5 sp, (sc in dc and ch-1 sp, picot) 9 times, sc in next dc, 5 sc in ch-5 sp**, in ch-3 sp work, (2 dc, picot) twice, 2 dc, rep from * around, end at ** on last rep; join with a sl st in 3rd ch of beg ch-3. Finish off; weave in ends.

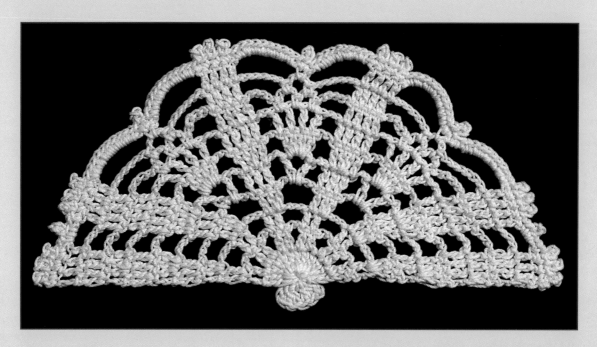

Fancy Pineapple

STITCH GUIDE

Beginning Block (beg block): Ch 3, turn; dc in next 3 dc.

Block: Dc in next 4 dc.

V-Stitch: In specified st work (dc, ch 3, dc).

Picot: Ch 3, sl st in sc at base of ch-3.

INSTRUCTIONS

Row 1: Ch 4, 4 dc in first ch, ch 3, rotate piece and sl st in first ch at base of dc just made; ch 3, 11 dc in ch; ch 3, turn.

Row 2: Dc in next dc; *ch 2, dc in next 2 dc; rep from * across; ch 3, turn.

Row 3: Dc in next dc; *ch 3, dc in next 2 dc, rep from * across ending with last dc in turning ch; ch 3, turn.

Row 4: Work 2 dc in next dc, ch 3; *(dc in next dc, 2 dc in next dc, ch 5) 3 times, dc in next dc, 2 dc in next dc; ch 3, 2 dc in next dc, dc in turning ch (counts as last dc); ch 3, turn.

Row 5: Dc in next 2 dc, ch 3; *(dc in next 3 dc, ch 2, V-st in ch-5 sp, ch 2) 3 times; (dc in next 3 dc, ch 3) twice, turn.

Row 6: Work 2 dc in next dc, dc in next dc, ch 3; *(dc in next dc, 2 dc in next dc, dc in next dc**, ch 2, 4 dc in V-st, ch 2) 3 times; rep from * to ** once more, ch 3, rep from * to ** once more.

Row 7: Beg block, ch 3; *[block, ch 2, (dc in next dc, ch 1) 3 times, dc in next dc, ch 2] 3 times, block, ch 3, block.

Row 8: Beg block, ch 3; *[block, ch 5, (sc in ch-1 sp, ch 3) twice, sc in next ch-1 sp, ch 5] 3 times, block, ch 3, block.

Row 9: Beg block, ch 3; *(block, ch 6, sc in ch-3 sp, ch 3, sc in next ch-3 sp, ch 6) 3 times, block, ch 3, block.

Row 10: Beg block, ch 3; *(block, ch 8, sc in ch-3 sp, ch 8) 3 times, block, ch 3, block; ch 1, turn.

Row 11: (Sc in dc, picot) 3 times, sc in next dc; ch 1, in ch-3 sp work (sc, picot, sc), ch 1; *(sc in next dc, picot) 3 times, sc in next dc, 10 sc in ch-8 sp; (sc, picot, sc) in sc, 10 sc in ch-8 sp; rep from * 2 times more; (sc in dc, picot) 3 times, sc in next dc, ch 1; in ch-3 sp work (sc, picot, sc), ch 1; (sc in dc, picot) 3 times, sc in next dc. Finish off; weave in ends.

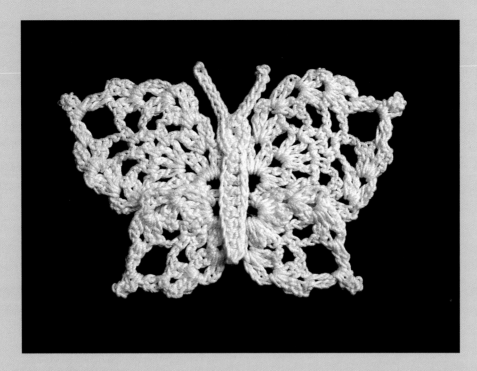

Pineapple Moth

STITCH GUIDE

Beginning Shell (beg shell): In specified sp work (ch 3, dc, ch 3, 2 dc).

Shell: In specified st work (2 dc, ch 2, 2 dc).

Picot: Ch 3, sl st in sc at base of ch-3.

Cluster (Cl): *(YO, insert hook in specified st and draw up a lp, YO and draw through 2 lps on hook) twice; YO and draw through rem lps on hook.

INSTRUCTIONS

Ch 2.

Rnd 1: In 2nd ch from hook work [(sc, ch 5) twice, (sc, ch 4) twice]; join with a sl st in first sc.

First Large Wing

Row 1: Sl st in ch-5 sp, work beg shell in same sp; ch 2, shell in same sp; ch 1, turn.

Row 2: Sl st in dc and ch-2 sp, beg shell in same sp; in next ch-2 sp work, (ch 1, dc) 4 times, ch 1, shell in shell; ch 1, turn.

Row 3: Sl st in dc and ch-2 sp, beg shell in same sp; ch 2, skip one ch-1 sp, (sc in next ch-1 sp, ch 2) 3 times, shell in shell; ch 1, turn.

Row 4: Sl st in dc and ch-2 sp, beg shell; ch 2, skip one ch-2 sp, (sc in next ch-2 sp, ch 2) twice, shell in shell; ch 1, turn.

Row 5: Sl st in dc and ch-2 sp, beg shell; ch 2, skip one ch-2 sp, sc in next ch-2 sp, ch 2, shell in shell; ch 1, turn.

Row 6: Sl st in dc and ch-2 sp, ch 2, dc, cl in next shell; ch 1, turn; work (sc, picot, sc) between cls; Finish off; weave in thread ends.

Second Large Wing: Attach thread to next ch-5 sp and rep Rows 1 through 6 of Large Wing.

First Small Wing

Row 1: Attach thread to any ch-4 sp; in same sp work [beg shell, (ch 2, sc) 3 times, ch 2, shell]; ch-1, turn.

Rows 2 to 4: Work same as Rows 4 through 6 of First Large Wing.

Body

Ch 14.

Row 1: Sc in 2nd ch from hook, sc in next ch, hdc in next 2 chs, dc in next 4 chs; hdc in next 2 chs, sc in next 2 chs, 4 sc in first ch; *ch 7, sl st in 2nd ch from hook and in next 5 chs, sl st in last sc made*, 2 sc in first ch; rep from * to * once more, 4 sc in first ch, sl st in base of next sc. Finish off; weave in thread ends. Sew body to butterfly center.

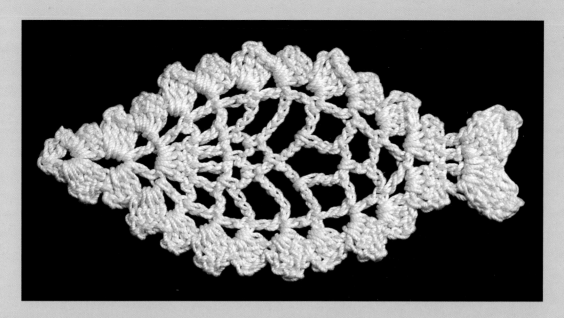

Pineapple Fish

STITCH GUIDE

V-stitch (V-st): In specified st work (dc, ch 3, dc).

Beginning Cluster (beg Cl): (YO, insert hook in next st, YO and draw up a lp, YO and draw through 2 lps on hook) 3 times, YO and draw through rem 4 lps on hook.

Cluster (Cl): (YO, insert hook in next st, YO and draw up a lp; YO and draw through 2 lps on hook) 4 times; YO and draw through rem 5 lps on hook.

INSTRUCTIONS

Ch 4.

Row 1: In 4th ch from hook work (dc, ch 3, 2 dc); ch 1, turn.

Row 2: Sl st in 2 dc and ch-3 sp; in ch-3 sp work (ch 3, 3 dc, ch 3, 4 dc); ch 1 turn.

Row 3: Sl st in 4 dc and ch-3 sp; in ch-3 sp work (ch 3, 3 dc, ch 2, V-st, ch 2, 4 dc); ch 1, turn.

Row 4: Sl st in 4 dc; ch 3, 3 dc in ch-2 sp, ch 2, dc in first dc of V-st, ch 2, 4 dc in V-st, ch 2, dc in next dc of V-st; ch 2, 3 dc in ch-2 sp, dc in next dc; ch 1, turn.

Row 5: Sl st in 4 dc; ch 3, 3 dc in ch-2 sp, ch 2, dc in dc, ch 2, (dc in next dc, ch-1) 3 times, (dc in next dc, ch 2) twice, 3 dc in ch-2 sp, dc in next dc; ch 1, turn work.

Row 6: Sl st in 4 dc; ch 3, 3 dc in ch-2 sp, ch 2, dc in dc; (ch 3, sc in ch-1 sp) 3 times, skip next dc, ch 3, dc in next dc; ch 2, 3 dc in ch-2 sp, dc in next dc; ch 1, turn.

Row 7: Sl st in 4 dc, ch 3, 3 dc in ch-2 sp, ch 2, dc in dc; ch 5, sc in ch-3 sp, ch 3, sc in next ch-3 sp, ch 5, dc in next dc; ch 2, 3 dc in ch-2 sp, dc in next dc; ch 1, turn.

Row 8: Sl st in 4 dc; ch 3, 3 dc in ch-2 sp, ch 2, dc in dc; ch 7, sc in ch-3 sp, ch 7, dc in next dc, ch 2, 3 dc in ch-2 sp, dc in next dc; ch 1, turn.

Row 9: Sl st in 4 dc; ch 3, 3 dc in ch-2 sp, ch 2, dc in dc, (ch 2, tr in ch-7 sp) twice; ch 2, dc in next dc, ch 2, 3 dc in ch-2 sp, dc in next dc; ch 1, turn.

Row 10: Sl st in 4 dc; ch 3, 3 dc in ch-2 sp, ch 2, dc in dc, ch 2; skip one ch-2 sp, dc in next ch-2 sp, ch 2, dc in next dc, ch 2, 3 dc in ch-2 sp, dc in next dc; ch 1, turn.

Row 11: Sl st in 4 dc; ch 3, 3 dc in ch-2 sp, ch 2, dc in dc; skip one dc, dc in next dc, ch 2, 3 dc in ch-2 sp, dc in next dc; ch 1, turn .

Row 12: Sl st in 4 dc; ch 3, (3 dc in ch-2 sp) twice, dc in next dc; ch 1, turn.

Row 13: Sl st in 3 dc, ch 3, dc in next 3 dc; ch 3, turn.

Row 14: Dc in last dc made, (3 dc in next dc) twice, 2 dc in top of turning ch: 10 sts; ch 2, turn.

Row 15: Beg Cl, hdc in next 2 sts, Cl. Finish off; weave in thread ends.

Pineapple Shining Star

STITCH GUIDE

Double V-Stitch (DV-st): In specified st [(dc, ch 3) twice, dc].

Picot-Cluster (picot-Cl): Ch 7, sl st in 2nd ch, ch 7, sl st in same place as last sl st; ch 5, sl st in same place as last sl st.

Picot: Ch 3, sl st in dc/sc.

INSTRUCTIONS

Ch 6; join with a sl st to form a ring.

Rnd 1: Ch 1, in ch-6 sp work, (sc, ch 5) 9 times, sc in same sp; ch 2, join with a dc in first sc.

Rnd 2: Ch 1, sc in join; *ch 5, sc in next ch-5 sp; rep from * around, ch 1, join with a tr in first sc.

Rnd 3: Ch 3, 3 dc in same sp as join; *ch 2, in next ch-5 sp work, (dc, ch 3, sc, ch 5, sc, ch 3, dc), ch 2**; 4 dc in next ch-5 sp; rep from * around, end at ** on last rep; join with a sl st in 3rd of beg ch-3.

Rnd 4: Ch 4 (count as dc and ch-1), (dc in next dc, ch 1) twice, dc in next dc; *ch 2, in next ch-5 sp work (dc, ch 3, sc, ch 5, sc, ch 3, dc), ch 2**; (dc in next dc, ch 1) 3 times, dc in next dc; rep from * around, end at ** on last rep; join with a sl st in 3rd ch of beg ch-3.

Rnd 5: Sl st in next 3 sts, ch 1, sc in same place as sl st, ch 3, sc in next ch-3 sp; *ch 5, in next ch-5 sp work, (dc, ch 3, sc, ch 5, sc, ch 3, dc), ch 5**; (sc in ch-1 sp, ch 3) twice, sc in next ch-1 sp; rep from * around, end at ** on last rep, sc in next ch-1 sp; ch 1, join with hdc in first sc.

Rnd 6: Ch 1, sc in join; *ch 3, sc in next ch-3 sp, ch 5, dc in next ch-3 sp, ch 3, DV-st in ch-5 sp, ch 3, dc in next ch-3 sp, ch 5**, sc in next ch-3 sp; rep from * around, end at ** on last repeat, join with a sl st in first sc.

Rnd 7: Sl st in next ch-3 st, ch 1; in same sp as join work *(sc, picot, sc); ch 9, skip one ch-3 sp, in next ch-3 sp work (dc, picot, dc), picot-Cl, ch 2; in next ch-3 sp work, (dc, picot, dc), ch 9, skip one ch-3 sp; rep from * around, join with a sl st in first sc. Finish off; weave in thread ends.

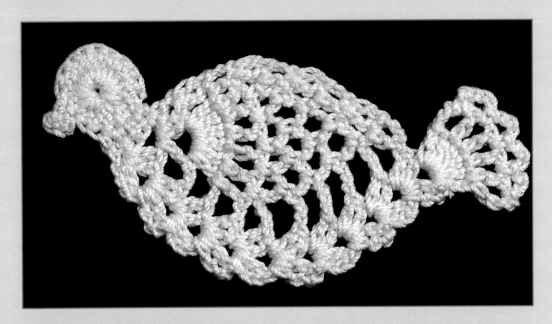

Pineapple in Flight

STITCH GUIDE

Beginning Shell (beg shell): In specified st work (ch 3, dc, ch 2, 2 dc).

Shell: In specified st work (2 dc, ch 2, 2 dc).

V-Stitch (V-st): In specified st work (dc, ch 3, dc).

INSTRUCTIONS

Ch 6; join with a sl st to form a ring.

Rnd 1: Ch 3 (counts as first dc), work 17 dc in ring; join with a sl st in 3rd ch of beg ch-3; ch 1, turn.

Note: *Remainder of pattern is worked in rows.*

Row 1: Sc in last dc of Rnd 1; hdc in next dc, dc in next 2 dc; ch 3, turn.

Row 2: In last dc of Row 1 work (dc, ch 2, 2 dc); ch 2, skip next 2 sts, 2 sc in next sc; ch 2, turn.

Row 3: Hdc in next sc, V-st in ch-2 sp, ch 2, shell in shell, ch 1, turn.

Row 4: Sl st in 2 dc and ch-2 sp, beg shell in same sp; ch 2, 6 dc in V-st, dc in hdc, dc in ch-2; ch 3, turn.

Row 5: Dc in next dc; (dc in next dc, ch 1) 6 times, shell in shell; ch 1, turn.

Row 6: Sl st in 2 dc and ch-2 sp, beg shell in same sp; ch 3, skip one ch-1 sp, (sc in next ch-1 sp, ch 3) 4 times; sc in next ch-1 sp, skip one dc, dc in next 2 dc; ch 3, turn.

Row 7: Dc in next dc; (sc in next ch-3 sp, ch 3) 4 times, shell in shell; ch 1, turn.

Row 8: Sl st in 2 dc and ch-2 sp, beg shell; ch 3, skip one ch-3 sp, (sc in next ch-3 sp, ch 3) twice, sc in next ch-3 sp, dc in 2 dc; ch 3, turn.

Row 9: Dc in dc, (sc in ch-3 sp, ch 3) twice, shell in shell; ch 1, turn.

Row 10: Sl st in 2 dc and ch-2 sp, beg shell; ch 3, skip one ch-3 sp, sc in next ch-3 sp, dc in 2 dc; ch 3, turn.

Row 11: Dc in next dc, shell in shell; ch 1, turn.

Row 12: Sl st in 2 dc and ch-2 sp, ch 3, 5 dc in ch-2 sp; ch 4, turn.

Row 13: (Dc in next dc, ch 1) 4 times, dc in 3rd ch of turning ch; ch 1, turn.

Row 14: Sl st in dc and ch-1 sp, (sc in ch-1 sp, ch 3) 4 times, sc in next ch-1 sp. Finish off; weave in thread ends.

Row 15 (beak): Attach thread to 6th dc of Rnd 1; ch 2, YO, insert hook in same place as join, YO and draw up a lp, YO and draw through 2 lps on hook; YO, insert hook in next dc, YO and draw up, a lp, YO and draw through 2 lps on hook, YO and draw through rem 3 lps on hook; Finish off; weave in thread ends.

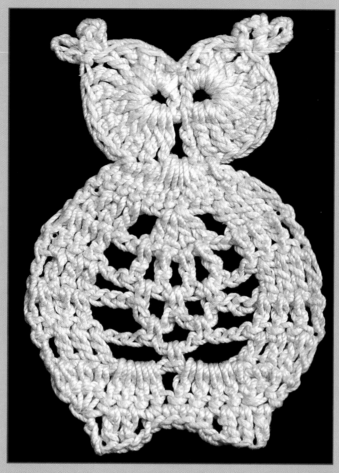

Pineapple Owl

STITCH GUIDE

Picot: Ch 4, sl st in last tr made.

Beginning Cluster (beg Cl): Ch 2, turn; *(YO, insert hook in next dc, YO and draw up a lp, YO and draw through 2 lps on hook) 3 times, YO and draw through rem lps on hook.

Cluster (Cl): (YO, insert hook in next dc, YO and draw up a lp, YO and draw through 2 lps on hook) 4 times, YO and draw through rem 5 lps on hook.

INSTRUCTIONS

Head (worked in rnds)

(Ch 6, join with a sl st to form a ring) twice: 2 rings side by side forming the head of the owl.

Rnd 1: Ch 4, in next ch-6 sp work (9 tr, 2 picot, tr, dc, hdc, sc); in next ch-6 sp work (sc, hdc, dc, 2 tr, 2 picot, 8 tr); join with a sl st in next tr, sl st in next tr; ch 3, turn.

Body (worked in rows)

Row 1: Dc in same st as turning ch, 2 dc in next tr, 5 dc between tr sts; (2 dc in next tr) twice, ch 3, turn work: 13 dc counting turning ch.

Row 2: Dc in next 3 dc, ch 2, skip 2 dc; 4 dc in next dc, ch 2, skip 2 dc, dc in next 4 dc; ch 3, turn work.

Row 3: Dc in next 3 dc, ch 2; (dc in next dc, ch 1) 3 times, dc in next dc, ch 2, dc in next 4 dc; ch 3, turn work.

Row 4: Dc in next 3 dc; (ch 3, sc in next ch-1 sp) 3 times, ch 3, dc in next 4 dc; ch 3, turn work.

Row 5: Dc in next 3 dc, ch 3, skip one ch-3 sp; (sc in next ch-3 sp, ch 3) twice, dc in next 4 dc; ch 3, turn work.

Row 6: Dc in next 3 dc, ch 3, skip one ch-3 sp, sc in next ch-3 sp, ch 3, skip next ch-3 sp, dc in next 4 dc.

Row 7: Work beg Cl; (4 dc in next ch-3 sp) twice, Cl; ch 3, turn work.

Row 8: Dc in next 2 sts, ch 2, sc in 4 sts, ch 2, dc in next 3 sts. Finish off; weave in thread ends.

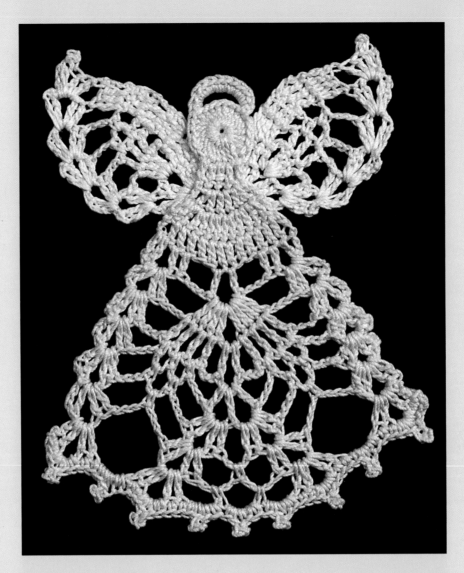

Pineapple Angel

STITCH GUIDE

Beginning Shell (beg shell): In specified st, work (ch 3, dc, ch 2, 2 dc).

Shell: In specified st, work (2 dc, ch 2, 2 dc).

Back Post Slip Stitch (bp sl st): Insert hook from back to front to back around post (vertical bar) of specified st in rnd below; YO and draw through lp on hook.

V-Stitch (V-st): In specified st, work (dc, ch 2, dc).

Double V-Stitch (DV-st): In specified st, work [(dc, ch 2) twice, dc].

Picot: Ch 3, sl st in last st made before ch-3.

INSTRUCTIONS

Starting at head, ch 6; join with a sl st in first ch to form a ring.

Rnd 1 (right side): Ch 3 (count as dc), 11 dc in ring, do not join; ch 6, turn; sl st in 7th dc from hook, sl st in next dc, turn; work 10 sc in ch-6 sp for halo, sl st in last dc made, 10 dc in ring; join with a sl st in 3rd ch of beg ch-3; ch 3 (counts as first dc on following row), turn.

Note: *Remainder of pattern is worked in rows.*

Row 1: Dc in next 4 dc, ch 3, turn.

Row 2: Work (2 dc in next dc) 3 times, dc in top of turning ch; ch 3, turn.

Row 3: Work (2 dc in next dc) 6 times, dc in next dc; ch 3, turn.

Row 4: Dc in next 13 dc; ch 3, turn.

Row 5: Dc in next dc, ch 2, dc in next 2 dc; ch 3, skip 2 dc, (dc in next dc, ch 3) twice; skip 2 dc, dc in next 2 dc, ch 2, dc in next 2 dc; ch 1, turn.

Row 6: Sl st in 2 dc and ch-2 sp, work beg shell; ch 3, skip one ch-3 sp; in next ch-3 sp work(4 dc, ch 3) twice, shell in next ch-2 sp; ch 1, turn.

Row 7: Sl st in 2 dc and ch-2 sp, work beg shell; ch 3, (dc in next dc, ch 1) 3 times, dc in next dc; ch 3, V-st in ch-3 sp, ch 3, (dc in next dc, ch 1) 3 times; dc in next dc, ch 3, shell in shell; ch 1, turn.

Row 8: Sl st in 2 dc and ch-2 sp, work beg shell; ch 3, (sc in ch-1 sp, ch 3) 3 times, DV-st in V-st, (ch 3, sc in next ch-1 sp) 3 times, ch 3, shell in shell; ch 1, turn.

Row 9: Sl st in 2 dc and ch-2 sp, work beg shell; ch 3, skip one ch-3 sp, (sc in next ch-3 sp, ch 3) twice; (shell in next ch-2 sp of double V-st, ch 3) twice, skip one ch-3 sp, (sc in next ch-3 sp, ch 3) twice, shell in shell; ch 1, turn.

Row 10: Sl st in 2 dc and ch-2 sp, work beg shell; ch 3, skip one ch-3 sp; *(sc in next ch-3 sp, ch 3, shell in next shell**, ch 3) twice; skip one ch-3 sp; rep from * to ** once more; ch 1, turn.

Row11: Sl st in 2 dc and ch-2 sp, work beg shell, ch 3, shell in next shell; (ch 3, sc in next ch-3 sp) twice, (ch 3, shell in next shell) twice; ch 1, turn.

Row 12: *Sc in 2 dc, in ch-2 sp work (2 sc, picot, 2 sc); sc in next 2 dc; in ch-3 sp work (2 sc, picot, 2 sc), sc in 2 dc; in ch-2 sp work, (2 sc, picot, 2 sc), sc in 2 dc* ; (in next ch-3 sp work 2 sc, picot, 2 sc) 3 times; rep from * to * once more. Finish off; weave in thread ends.

First Wing

Row 1: Attach yarn to wrong side of work with a bp sl st in 3rd dc on right-hand side of Row 3; ch 5, bp sl st in 3rd dc of row 1; ch 5, bp sl st in 3rd dc on left side of Row 3; sl st in ch-5 sp, turn.

Row 2: In ch-5 sp work (beg shell, ch 3, 4 dc); ch 3, turn.

Row 3: Dc in next 3 dc, ch 2, 3 dc in next ch-3 sp, ch 2, shell in shell; ch 1, turn.

Row 4: Sl st in 2 dc and ch-2 sp; work beg shell in same sp; ch 2, (dc in next dc of 3-dc group, ch 1) 3 times, dc in next 4 dc; ch 3, turn.

Row 5: Dc in next 3 dc, ch 1, skip one ch-1 sp; (sc in next ch-1 sp, ch 3) twice, shell in shell; ch 1, turn.

Row 6: Sl st in 2 dc and ch-2 sp, work beg shell in same sp; ch 3, skip one ch-3 sp, sc in next ch-3 sp, ch 1, dc in next 4 dc; ch 3, turn.

Row 7: Dc in next 3 dc, shell in shell, ch 1, turn.

Row 8: Sl st in 2 dc and ch-2 sp; (ch 3, dc, picot, 2 dc) in shell; skip 3 dc, sc in next dc. Finish off; weave in thread ends.

Second Wing

Join thread in next ch-5 sp on wrong side. Repeat Rows 1 through 8 of first wing. Finish off; weave in thread ends.

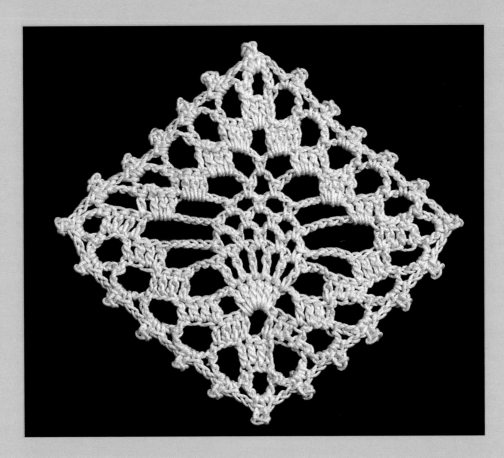

Petite Pineapple

STITCH GUIDE

Beginning Block Increase (beg block inc): Ch 6, turn; dc in 5th ch from hook, dc in next ch, dc in next dc.

End Block Increase (end block inc): Dc in last dc of previous row; [YO, insert hook in base of last dc made, YO and draw through one loop, (YO and draw through 2 lps) twice] 3 times.

Picot: Ch 3, sl st in sc.

INSTRUCTIONS

Row 1: Ch 7; dc in 5th ch from hook, dc in next 2 ch sts.

Row 2: Beg block inc; ch 2, end block inc.

Row 3: Beg block inc; ch 2, 6 dc in ch-2 sp, ch 2, end block inc.

Row 4: Beg block inc, ch 3; (dc in dc, ch 1) 5 times, dc in next dc, ch 3, end block inc.

Row 5: Beg block inc, ch 5; (sc in ch-1 sp, ch 3) 4 times, sc in next ch-1 sp, ch 5, end block inc.

Row 6: Beg block inc; ch 7; (sc in ch 3 sp, ch 3) 3 times, sc in next ch-3 sp, ch 7, end block inc; ch 1, turn.

Row 7: Sl st in 4 dc; ch 3, 3 dc in ch-7 sp, ch 5; (sc in ch-3 sp, ch 3) twice, sc in next ch-3 sp, ch 5, 3 dc in ch-7 sp, dc in next dc; ch 1, turn.

Row 8: Sl st in 4 dc; ch 3, 3 dc in ch-5 sp; ch 5, sc in ch-3 sp, ch 3, sc in next ch-3 sp, ch 5; 3 dc in ch-5 sp, dc in next dc; ch 1, turn.

Row 9: Sl st in 4 dc; ch 3, 3 dc in ch-5 sp; ch 3, sc in ch-3 sp, ch 3, 3 dc in ch-5 sp, dc in next dc; ch 1, turn.

Row 10: Sl st in 4 dc; ch 3, 3 dc in ch-3 sp, ch 2, 3 dc in ch-3 sp, dc in next dc; ch 1, turn .

Row 11: Sl st in 4 dc; ch 3, 2 dc in ch-3 sp, dc in next dc.

Note: *Remainder of pattern is worked in rounds.*

Rnd 1: Ch 1, sc in dc; (ch 5, sc in top of outside st of next block) 5 times; ch 5, sc in base of same dc; *(ch 5, sc in base of outside dc of next block) 5 times**, ch 5, skip 2 dc, sc in base of same dc, rep from * to ** once more; ch 5, sc in top of same dc, (ch 5, sc in top of outside st of next block) 5 times; ch 2; join with a dc in first sc.

Rnd 2: Ch 1, (sc, picot, sc) in same space as join; *ch 2, (sc, picot, sc) in next ch-5 sp; rep from * around; ch 2, join with a sl st in first sc. Finish off; weave in ends.

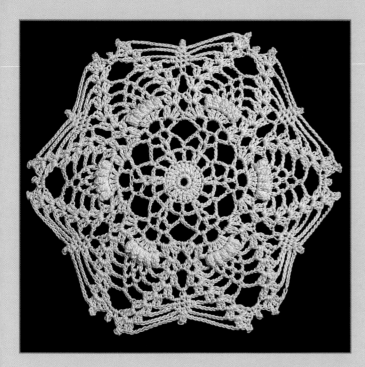

Pineapple Cobweb

STITCH GUIDE

Beginning Shell (beg shell): In specified st work (ch 3, dc, ch 2, 2 dc).

Shell: In specified st, work (2 dc, ch 2, 2 dc).

Beginning V-Stitch (beg V-st): In same place as join, work ch 6, dc.

V-Stitch (V-st): In specified st work (dc, ch 3, dc).

Double V-Stitch (DV-st): In specified st work (dc, ch 3) twice, dc in same st.

Popcorn stitch (PC): In specified st work 4 dc; remove lp from hook, insert hook from front to back in top of first dc, pick up dropped lp and draw lp through.

Picot: Ch 3, sl st in last st made before ch-3.

Large Picot: Ch 6, sl st in dc.

INSTRUCTIONS

Ch 6, join with a sl st to form a ring.

Rnd 1: Ch 1, 12 sc in ring; join with a sl st in first sc.

Rnd 2: Ch 3 (count as dc), dc in join; *2 dc in next sc; rep from * around, join with a sl st in 3rd ch of ch-3.

Rnd 3: Ch 6 (count as dc and ch-3), *skip one dc, in next dc work (dc, large picot, dc), ch 3** skip one dc, dc in next dc, ch 3; rep from * around, end at ** on last rep; join with a sl st in 3rd ch of ch-3. Finish off, weave in thread end.

Rnd 4: Attach thread to any large picot, ch 6, V-st in large picot; *ch 3, sc in next dc, ch 3**, DV-st in next large picot; rep from * around, end at ** on last rep; join with a sl st in 3rd ch of ch-6.

Rnd 5: Sl st in ch-3 sp, beg V-st; *ch 3, V-st in next ch-3 sp** ch 3, skip 2 ch-3 sps, V-st in next ch-3 sp; rep from * around, end at ** on last rep; ch 1, join with hdc in 3rd ch of ch-6.

Rnd 6: Ch 1, sc in join; *shell in V-st, ch 2, 5 dc in next ch-3 sp, ch 2, shell in next V-st** sc in ch-3 sp; rep from * around, end at ** on last rep, join with a sl st in first sc.

Rnd 7: Sl st in 2 dc and ch-2 sp, beg shell; *ch 2, (PC in next dc of 5-dc group, ch 1) 4 times, PC in next dc; ch 2, (shell in next shell**) twice; rep from * around, end at ** on last rep, join with a sl st in 3rd ch of ch-3.

Rnd 8: Sl st in dc and ch-2 sp, beg shell; *(ch 3, sc in ch-1 sp) 4 times, (ch 3, shell in next shell**) twice; rep from * around, end at ** on last rep; ch 3, join with a sl st in 3rd ch of ch-3.

Rnd 9: Sl st in dc and ch-2 sp, beg shell; *ch 3, skip one ch-3 sp, (sc in ch-3 sp, ch 3) 3 times, shell in next shell, ch 3, sc in next ch-3 sp, ch 3**, shell in next shell; rep from * around, end at ** on last rep, join with a sl st in 3rd ch of ch-3.

Rnd 10: Sl st in dc and ch-2 sp, beg shell; *ch 3, skip one ch-3 sp, (sc in ch-3 sp, ch 3) twice, shell in next shell; ch 4, sc in ch-3 sp, sc in sc, sc in next ch-3 sp, ch 4**, shell in next shell; rep from * around, end at ** on last rep, join with a sl st in 3rd ch of ch-3.

Rnd 11: Sl st in dc and ch-2 sp, beg shell; *ch 3, skip one ch-3 sp, sc in ch-3 sp, ch 3, shell in next shell; ch 5, sc in ch-4 sp, sc in 3 sc, sc in next ch-4 sp, ch 5**, shell in next shell; rep from * around, end at ** on last rep; join with a sl st in 3rd ch of ch-3.

Rnd 12: Sl st in dc and ch-2 sp, beg shell; *ch 3, shell in next shell, ch 9, skip one sc, sc in 3 sc, ch 9**, shell in next shell; rep from * around, end at ** on last rep, join with a sl st in 3rd ch of ch-3.

Rnd 13: Sl st in dc and ch-2 sp, ch 3, dc, picot, 2 dc; *in ch-3 sp work (sc, picot, sc), in next shell work (2 dc, picot, 2 dc); ch 11, skip one sc, in next sc work, (sc, picot sc) ch 11**, in next shell work, (2 dc, picot, 2 dc); rep from * around, end at ** on last rep; join with a sl st in 3rd ch of ch-3. Finish off; weave in thread ends.

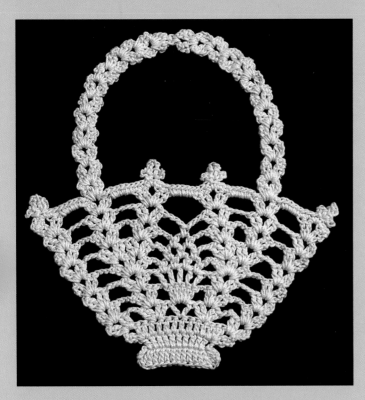

Pineapple Basket

STITCH GUIDE

Beginning Shell (beg shell): In specified st work (ch 3, dc, ch 2, 2 dc).

Shell: In specified st work (2 dc, ch 2, 2 dc).

Double shell (d-shell): In specified st work [(2 dc, ch 2) twice, 2 dc].

V-Stitch (V-st): (Dc, ch 2, dc) in specified st.

Picot Cluster (picot-Cl): In last sc made work, (ch 3, sl st, ch 5, sl st, ch 3, sl st).

INSTRUCTIONS

Ch 14.

Row 1: Work 2 dc in 4th ch from hook, dc in next 9 chs; in next ch st work (3 dc, ch 3, sl st), ch 3; working on opposite side of beg ch, dc in next 9 unused lps, dc in next st; ch 3, turn.

Row 2: In dc work (dc, ch 2, 2 dc), dc in next 9 dc, shell in next dc; ch 1, turn.

Row 3: Sl st in 2 dc and ch-2 sp, beg shell; ch 3, skip 3 dc, shell in next dc, skip 2 dc, V-st in next dc; skip 2 dc, shell in next dc, ch 3, shell in next ch-2 sp; ch 1, turn.

Row 4: Sl st in 2 dc and ch-2 sp, beg shell; ch 3, shell in shell, ch 2, 5 dc in V-st; ch 2, shell in shell, ch 3, shell in shell; ch 1, turn.

Row 5: Sl st in 2 dc and ch-2 sp, beg shell; ch 3, shell in shell, (ch 1, dc in next dc of 5-dc group) 5 times, ch 1, shell in shell, ch 3, shell in shell; ch 1, turn.

Row 6: Sl st in 2 dc and ch-2 sp, beg shell; ch 3, d-shell in next shell, ch 3, skip one ch-1 sp, (sc in next ch-1 sp, ch 3) 4 times; d-shell in shell, ch 3, shell in shell; ch 1, turn.

Row 7: Sl st in 2 dc and ch-2 sp, beg shell; ch 3, (shell in ch-2 sp) twice, ch 3, skip one ch-3 sp; (sc in next ch-3 sp) 3 times, (shell in ch-2 sp) twice, ch 3, shell in shell; ch 1, turn.

Row 8: Sl st in 2 dc and ch-2 sp, beg shell; (ch 3, shell in shell) twice, ch 3, skip one ch-3 sp, (sc in next ch-3 sp, ch 3) twice; (shell in shell, ch 3) twice, shell in shell; ch 1, turn.

Row 9: Sl st in 2 dc and ch-2 sp, beg shell; (ch 3, shell in shell) twice, ch 3, skip one ch-3 sp, sc in next ch-3 sp, (ch 3, shell in shell) 3 times; ch 1, turn.

Row 10: Sl st in 2 dc and ch-2 sp, beg shell; (ch 3, shell in shell) 5 times; ch 1, turn.

Row 11: Sc in 2 dc, in ch-2 sp work (sc, picot-Cl, sc), 5 sc in ch-3 sp, sl st in next 6 sts; *5 sc in next ch-3 sp, sc in next 2 dc, in ch-2 sp work, (sc, picot-Cl, sc), sc in 2 dc; rep from * once more; 5 sc in ch-3 sp, sl st in next 6 sts, 5 sc in ch-3 sp, sc in 2 dc, in ch-2 sp work (sc, picot-Cl, sc), sc in 2 dc. Finish off; weave in thread ends.

Handle

Attach thread to 2nd shell of Row 11; (beg shell, ch-1, turn; sl st in 2 dc and ch-2 sp) 11 times, beg shell. Finish off; weave in thread ends.

Attach thread to 2nd shell on opposite edge of Row 11; (beg shell, ch-1 turn, sl st in 2 dc and ch-2 sp) 11 times, ch 3, dc in shell, 2 sc in ch-2 sp of 12th shell of first handle section, 2 dc. Finish off; weave in thread ends.

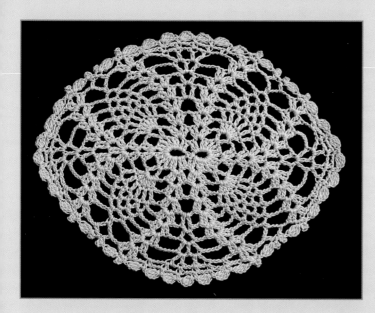

Pineapple Cluny Leaves

STITCH GUIDE

Beginning Shell (beg shell): In specified st work (ch 3, dc, ch 2, 2 dc).

Shell: In specified st work (2 dc, ch 2, 2 dc).

Double Shell (d-shell): In specified st work [(2 dc, ch 2) twice, 2 dc].

Double V-st (DV-st): In specified st, work [(dc, ch 1) twice, dc].

V Stitch (V-st): In specified st or sp work (dc, ch 2, dc).

Cluny Leaf: Ch 4, (YO, insert hook in first ch, YO and draw up a lp, YO and draw through 2 lps on hook) twice, YO and draw through rem lps on hook.

Picot: Ch 3, sl st in last st made.

INSTRUCTIONS

Rnd 1: (Ch 10; join with a sl st in first ch to form ring) twice; sl st in ch-10 sp, beg shell; in same ch-10 sp work, (ch 1, V-st, ch 1, shell) twice; in next ch-10 sp work, (shell, ch 1, V-st, ch 1) twice, shell in same sp; join with a sl st in 3rd ch of ch-3.

Rnd 2: Sl st in dc and ch-2 sp, beg shell; *(ch 2, V-st in V-st, ch 2, shell in shell) twice**, shell in next shell; rep from * to ** once more; join with a sl st in 3rd ch of ch-3.

Rnd 3: Sl st in 2 dc and ch-2 sp, beg shell; (ch 2, 6 dc in V-st, ch 2, shell in shell) twice; (ch 2, shell in next shell, ch 2, 6 dc in V-st) twice; ch 2, shell in next shell, ch 2; join with a sl st in 3rd ch of ch-3.

Rnd 4: Sl st in 2 dc and ch-2 sp, beg shell; *(ch 1, dc in next dc of 6-dc group) 6 times, ch 1**, d-shell in shell; rep from * to ** once more; shell in next shell, ch 3***, shell in next shell; rep from * once more; ending at ***; join with a sl st in 3rd ch of ch-3.

Rnd 5: Sl st in 2 dc and ch-2 sp, beg shell; *ch 3, skip one ch-1 sp, (sc in next ch-1 sp, ch 3) 5 times**; shell in ch-2 sp, ch 2, shell in next ch-2 sp; rep from * to ** once more, shell in next shell, ch 2, V-st in ch-3 sp, ch 2***, shell in shell; rep from * once more, ending at ***; join with a sl st in 3rd ch of ch-3.

Rnd 6: Sl st in 2 dc and ch-2 sp, beg shell; *ch 3, skip one ch-3 sp, (sc in next ch-3 sp, ch 3) 4 times, shell in shell; ch 2, V-st in ch-2 sp, ch 2, shell in shell, ch 3, skip one ch-3 sp; (sc in next ch-3 sp, ch 3) 4 times, shell in next shell, ch 2, V-st in V-st, ch 2**, shell in next shell; rep from * once more, ending at **; join with a sl st in 3rd ch of ch-3.

Rnd 7: Sl st in 2 dc and ch-2 sp, beg shell; *ch 3, skip one ch-3 sp, (sc in next ch-3 sp, ch 3) 3 times, shell in shell; ch 5, DV-st in V-st, ch 5**, shell in next shell; rep from * around, ending at **; join with a sl st in 3rd ch of ch-3.

Rnd 8: Sl st in 2 dc and ch-2 sp, beg shell; *ch 3, skip one ch-3 sp, (sc in next ch-3 sp, ch 3) twice, shell in shell; ch 5, V-st in next V-st, ch 2, V-st in next ch-2 sp, ch 5**, shell in next shell; rep from * around, ending at ** ; join with a sl st in 3rd ch of ch-3.

Rnd 9: Sl st in 2 dc and ch-2 sp, beg shell; *ch 5, skip one ch-3 sp, sc in next ch-3 sp, ch 5, shell in shell; ch 3, sc in ch-5 sp, (ch 3, sc in dc) 4 times, ch 3, sc in ch-5 sp, ch 3**, shell in next shell; rep from * around, end at **; join with a sl st in 3rd ch of ch-3.

Rnd 10: Sl st in 2 dc and ch-2 sp, ch 1; *in shell work, (sc, picot, sc), work cluny leaf, picot; (dc in ch-5 sp) twice, picot, cluny leaf; in next shell work, (sc, picot, sc), (cluny leaf, sc in next sc) 6 times, cluny leaf; rep from * around; join with a sl st in first sc. Finish off; weave in thread ends.

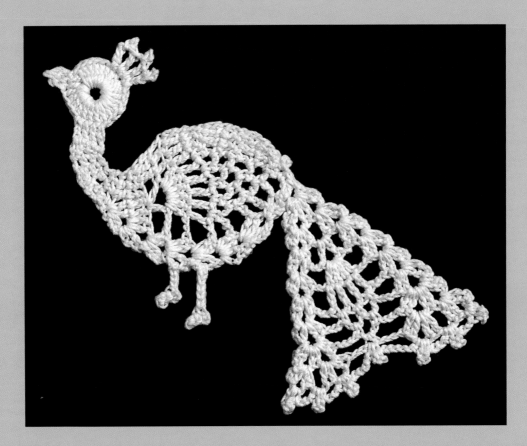

Pineapple Peacock

STITCH GUIDE

Beginning Shell (beg shell): In specified sp work (ch 3, dc, ch 2, 2 dc).

Shell: In specified st work (2 dc, ch 2, 2 dc).

Beginning double Shell (beg d-shell): In specified sp work [ch 3, dc, (ch 2, 2 dc) twice].

Double shell (d-shell): In specified st work [(2 dc, ch 2) twice, 2 dc].

Picot: Ch 3, sl st in sc.

V-Stitch (V-st): In specified st work (dc, ch 2, dc).

INSTRUCTIONS

Starting at head, ch 8, join with a sl st to form a ring.

Rnd 1: Ch 3 (counts as first dc of rnd), 23 dc in ring; join with a sl st in 3rd ch of ch-3.

Beak: Ch 3, (YO, insert hook in next dc, YO and draw up a lp, YO and draw through 2 lps on hook) twice: 3 lps now on hook; (YO and draw through 2 lps) twice. Finish off; weave in thread ends.

Note: *Remainder of pattern is worked in rows.*

Row 1: To work comb, attach thread to 16th dc of Rnd 1; ch 6, sl st in 4th ch from hook; (ch 1, dc in next dc, picot) twice, ch 1, dc in next dc. Finish off; weave in thread ends.

Row 2 (neck): Attach thread to 7th dc of Rnd 1; ch 3, dc in next 3 dc; ch 1, turn.

Row 3: Sc in dc, hdc in next dc, dc in next 2 dc; ch 3, turn.

Row 4: Dc in next dc, hdc in hdc, sc in sc; ch 1, turn.

Row 5 through 7: Rep Rows 3, 4 and 3 in that order.

Row 8: (Dc, ch 2, 2 dc) in dc, dc in next dc, hdc in next hdc, sc in sc; ch 1, turn.

Row 9: Sc in sc, hdc in hdc, dc in next 3 dc, shell in shell; ch 1, turn.

Row 10 (body): Sl st in 2 dc and ch-2 sp, work beg shell in same sp; ch 2, skip 2 dc, V-st in next dc, skip 2 dc, dc in next st, 2 dc in last st; ch 3, turn.

Row 11: Dc in next 2 dc, 6 dc in V-st, ch 2, shell in shell; ch 1, turn.

Row 12: Sl st in 2 dc and ch-2 sp, work beg shell in same sp; *(ch 1, dc in next dc of 6-dc group) 6 times, dc in next 3 dc; ch 3, turn.

Row 13: Dc in next 2 dc; *(sc in ch-1 sp, ch 3) 5 times, shell in shell; ch 1, turn.

Row 14: Sl st in 2 dc and ch-2 sp, work beg shell in same sp; ch 3, skip one ch-3 sp, (sc in next ch-3 sp, ch 3) 3 times, sc in next ch-3 sp, dc in next 3 dc; ch 3, turn.

Row 15: Dc in next 2 dc; (sc in ch-3 sp, ch 3) 3 times, 2 sc in shell; ch 1, turn work.

Row 16: Sc in 2 sc, ch 3, skip one ch-3 sp, sc in next ch-3 sp, ch 3, sc in next ch-3 sp, dc in 3 dc; ch 3, turn.

Row 17: Dc in next 2 dc, sc in ch-3 sp, ch 3, sc in last 2 sc; ch 3, turn.

Row 18: Dc in next sc, sc in ch-3 sp, sc in sc, skip 2 dc, sc in next dc; ch-1, turn.

Row 19 (tail): Sl st in next 4 sts, sl st around post of dc, beg d-shell around turning ch, ch 1, turn.

Row 20: Sl st in 2 dc and ch-2 sp, beg shell in same sp, ch 3, shell in next ch-2 sp; ch 1, turn.

Row 21: Sl st in 2 dc and ch-2 sp, beg shell in same sp; ch 2, V-st in ch-3 sp, ch 2, shell in next shell; ch 1, turn.

Row 22: Sl st in 2 dc and ch-2 sp, beg shell in same sp; ch 2, 4 dc in V-st, ch 2, shell in next shell; ch 1, turn.

Row 23: Sl st in 2 dc and ch-2 sp, beg shell in same sp; ch 2, (dc in next dc of 4-dc group, ch 1) 3 times, dc in next dc, ch 2, shell in next shell; ch 1, turn.

Row 24: Sl st in 2 dc and ch-2 sp, beg shell in same sp; (ch 3, sc in ch-1 sp) 3 times, ch 3, shell in next shell; ch 1, turn.

Row 25: Sl st in 2 dc and ch-2 sp, beg d-shell in same sp; ch 3, skip one ch-3 sp, (sc in next ch-3 sp, ch 3) twice, d-shell in next shell; ch 1, turn.

Row 26: Sl st in 2 dc and ch-2 sp, beg shell in same sp; ch 2, shell in next ch-2 sp, ch 3, skip one ch-3 sp, sc in next ch-3 sp, ch 3, shell in ch-2 sp, ch 2, shell in next ch-2 sp; ch 1, turn.

Row 27: Sl st in 2 dc and ch-2 sp, ch 1; *in shell work, (sc, picot, sc), ch 3; in ch-2 sp work, (sc, picot, sc, ch 3); in next shell work, (sc, picot, sc)**, ch 5, in next sc work (sc, picot, sc), ch 5; rep from * to ** once more. Finish off; weave in thread ends.

Legs

Front Leg

Attach thread around post of end dc of shell of Row 11; ch 8, sl st in 4th ch from hook, ch 3, sl st in same place as last sl st, sl st in each of next 4 chs. Finish off; weave in thread ends.

Back Leg

Attach thread around post of end dc of shell of Row 12; ch 10, sl st in 4th ch from hook, ch 3, sl st in same place as last sl st, sl st in each of next 6 ch sts. Finish off; weave in thread ends.

Pineapple Twins

STITCH GUIDE

Beginning Shell (beg shell): In specified sp work (ch 3, dc, ch 2, 2 dc).

Shell: In specified st work (2 dc, ch 2, 2 dc).

V Stitch (V-st): In specified st work (dc, ch 3, dc).

Cluster (Cl): YO, insert hook in ch-3 sp, YO and draw up a lp, YO and draw through 2 lps on hook; YO, insert hook in next ch-3 sp, YO and draw up a lp, YO and draw through 2 lps on hook, YO and draw through rem lps on hook.

Popcorn stitch (PC): In specified st work 4 dc; drop lp from hook, insert hook from front to back in top of first dc; pick up dropped lp and draw through lp on hook.

Picot: Ch 3, sl st in dc.

INSTRUCTIONS

First Pineapple

Ch 39.

Row 1 (right side): Sl st in 7th ch from hook; *ch 3, skip three chs, sl st in next ch; rep from * across, sl st in first ch; ch 1 turn.

Row 2: Sl st in ch-sp, beg shell in same sp, ch 3, skip one ch-sp, shell in next ch-sp, ch 3, skip one ch-sp, V-st in next ch-sp, (ch 3, skip one ch-sp, shell in next ch-sp) twice; ch 1, turn.

Row 3: Sl st in 2 dc and ch-2 sp, beg shell; ch 3, shell in shell, ch 3, 8 dc in V-st, (ch 3, shell in next shell) twice; ch 1, turn.

Row 4: Sl st in 2 dc and ch-2 sp, beg shell; ch 3, shell in next shell, (ch 1, dc in next dc of 8-dc group) 8 times, ch 1, shell in next shell, ch 3, shell in next shell; ch 1, turn.

Row 5: Sl st in 2 dc and ch-2 sp, beg shell; ch 3, shell in next shell, ch 3, skip one ch-1 sp, (PC in next ch-1 sp, ch 3) 7 times, shell in next shell, ch 3, shell in next shell; ch 1, turn.

Row 6: Sl st in 2 dc and ch-2 sp, beg shell; ch 3, shell in next shell, ch 3, skip one ch-3 sp, (sc in next ch-3 sp, ch 3) 6 times, shell in next shell, ch 3, shell in next shell; ch 1, turn.

Row 7: Sl st in 2 dc and ch-2 sp, beg shell; ch 3, shell in next shell, ch 3, skip one ch-3 sp, (PC in next ch-3 sp, ch 3) 5 times, shell in next shell, ch 3, shell in next shell; ch 1, turn.

Row 8: Sl st in 2 dc and ch-2 sp, beg shell; ch 3, shell in next shell, ch 3, skip one ch-3 sp, (sc in next ch-3 sp, ch 3) 4 times, shell in next shell, ch 3, shell in next shell; ch 1, turn.

Row 9: Sl st in 2 dc and ch-2 sp, beg shell; ch 3, shell in next shell, ch 3, skip one ch-3 sp, (PC in next ch-3 sp, ch 3) 3 times, shell in next shell, ch 3, shell in next shell; ch 1, turn.

Row 10: Sl st in 2 dc and ch-2 sp, beg shell; ch 3, shell in next shell, ch 3, skip one ch-3 sp, (sc in next ch-3 sp, ch 3) twice, shell in next shell, ch 3, shell in next shell; ch 1, turn.

Row 11: Sl st in 2 dc and ch-2 sp, beg shell; ch 3, shell in next shell, ch 3, skip one ch-3 sp, PC in next ch-3 sp, (ch 3, shell in next shell) twice; ch 1, turn.

Row 12: Sl st in 2 dc and ch-2 sp, beg shell; ch 3, shell in next shell, Cl, shell in next shell, ch 3, shell in next shell; ch 1, turn.

Row 13: Sl st in 2 dc and ch-2 sp, beg shell; ch 3, (2 dc in next shell) twice, ch 3, shell in next shell; ch 1, turn.

Row 14: Sl st in 2 dc and ch-2 sp, beg shell; ch 3, shell in next shell; ch 1, turn.

Row 15: Sl st in 2 dc and ch-2 sp, ch 3, dc; sc in ch-3 sp, 2 dc in next shell. Finish off; weave in thread ends.

Second Pineapple

Attach thread on wrong side of first row; with right side facing for Row 1, rep Rows 1 through 15. At end of Row 15, do not finish off.

Border

Rnd 1: Ch 1, sc in dc; *(ch 7, skip one row, sc in first dc of next row) 6 times, ch 7, sc in next ch sp of row 1, (ch 7, skip one row, sc in first dc of next row) 7 times, ch 3**, sc in first dc of next row, rep from * to ** once more, sl st in first sc.

Rnd 2: Ch 6, (dc, picot, ch 3, dc) in join, sc in ch-7 sp; *in next sc work (dc, ch 3, dc, picot, ch 3, dc), sc in ch-7 sp; rep from * around, sl st in 3rd ch of ch-6. Finish off; weave in thread ends.

Pineapple Water Lily

STITCH GUIDE

Beginning Shell (beg shell): In specified st work (ch 3, dc, ch 2, 2 dc).

Shell: In specified st work (2 dc, ch 2, 2 dc).

Picot: Ch 3, sl st in sc.

Cluster (Cl): *(YO insert hook in specified st, YO and draw up a lp, YO and draw through 2 lps on hook) twice, YO and draw through rem 3 lps on hook.

INSTRUCTIONS

Flower Center

Ch 6; join with a sl st to form a ring.

Rnd 1 (right side): Ch 1, work 18 sc in ring; join with a sc in first sc.

Rnd 2: *Ch 5, skip 2 sc, sc in next sc; rep from * around, ending last rep with ch 5; join with a sl st in first sc: 6 ch-5 lps.

Rnd 3: Working behind Rnd 2, ch 1, sc in next sc on Rnd 1; *ch 5, sc in first of next 2 skipped sc on Rnd 1; rep from * around, ch 5, join with a sl st in first sc: 6 ch-5 lps.

Rnd 4: Working behind Rnd 3, ch 1, sc in next skipped sc on Rnd 1; *ch 5, sc in next skipped sc on Rnd 1; rep from * around; join with a sl st in first sc: 6 ch-5 lps. Finish off, weave in ends.

Petals

Note: *Petals are worked individually in rows.*

Top Petal Round

First Petal

Row 1: With right side facing, join thread to any ch-5 sp of Rnd 2; in same sp work beg shell, (ch 2, sc) 3 times, ch 2, shell; ch 1; turn.

Row 2: Sl st in dc and ch-2 sp, beg shell in same sp; ch 2, skip one ch-2 sp; (sc in next ch-2 sp, ch 2) twice, shell in shell; ch 1, turn.

Row 3: Sl st in dc and ch-2 sp, beg shell in same sp; ch 2, skip one ch-2 sp, sc in next ch-2 sp, ch 2, shell in shell; ch 1, turn.

Row 4: Sl st in dc and ch-2 sp, ch 2, Cl in next shell, 2 Cl in next shell; ch1, turn.

Row 5: Work (sc, picot, sc) between clusters. Finish off; weave in thread ends.

(Join thread in next ch-5 sp of Rnd 2 and work same as First Petal) 5 times more. At end, finish off; weave in thread ends.

Center Petal Round

Second Petal

Row 1: Join thread in any ch-5 sp of Rnd 3; in same sp work (beg shell, ch 2, shell); ch 1, turn.

Row 2: Sl st in dc and ch-2 sp, beg shell in same sp; in next ch-2 sp work (ch 1, dc) 4 times, ch 1, shell in shell; ch 1, turn.

Row 3: Sl st in dc and ch-2 sp, beg shell in same sp; ch 2, skip one ch-1 sp, (sc in next ch-1 sp, ch 2) 3 times, shell in shell; ch 1, turn.

Row 4: Sl st in dc and ch-2 sp, beg shell in same sp; ch 2, skip one ch-2 sp, (sc in next ch-2 sp, ch 2) twice, shell in shell; ch 1, turn.

Row 5: Sl st in dc and ch-2 sp, work beg shell in same sp; ch 2, skip one ch-2 sp, sc in next ch-2 sp, ch 2, shell in shell; ch 1, turn.

Row 6: Sl st in dc and ch-2 sp, ch 2, Cl in first shell, 2 Cl in next shell, ch 1, turn.

Row 7: Repeat Row 5 of First Petal.

(Join thread in next ch-5 sp of Rnd 3 and work same as Second Petal) 5 times; At end, finish off; weave in thread ends.

Bottom Petal Round

Join thread in any ch-5 sp of Rnd 4; complete each petal following instructions for Second Petal.

Pineapple Lady

STITCH GUIDE

Beginning Shell (beg shell): In specified space work (ch 3, dc, ch 2, 2 dc).

Shell: In specified space work (2 dc, ch 2, 2 dc).

Double Shell (d-shell): In specified st work [(2 dc, ch 2) twice, 2 dc].

Beginning double Shell (beg d-shell): In specified sp work [ch 3, dc, (ch 2, 2 dc) twice].

V Stitch (V-st): In specified st work (dc, ch 3, dc).

Picot: Ch 4, sl st in first ch.

INSTRUCTIONS

Starting at top of hat, ch 4; join with a sl st to form a ring.

Rnd 1 (right side): Ch 3, work 12 dc in ring.

Note: *Remainder of piece is worked in rows.*

Row 1: Ch 3; insert hook from front to back to front around post (vertical bar) of last dc made and work 5 dc around post; 4 dc in ring; skip beg ch-3, work 6 dc around post of first dc of Rnd 1; ch 1, turn.

Row 2 (hat ruffle): Sc in first dc; *ch 3, sc in back lp of next dc; rep from * across. Finish off; weave in thread ends.

Row 3 (neck): Attach thread to 5th dc of Row 1; ch 7, skip 5 dc, dc in back lp of next dc of Row 1; ch 3, turn: neck lp made.

Row 4 (blouse): Work 10 dc in ch-7 sp, dc in 3rd ch of ch-7; ch 4, turn.

Row 5: (Dc in next dc, ch 1) 10 times, dc in next dc; ch 5, turn.

Row 6: (Dc in next dc, ch 2) 10 times, dc in next dc; ch 1, turn.

Row 7: *Sc in dc, ch 3, sc in ch-2 sp, ch 3; rep from * across, ending sc in next dc. Finish off; weave in thread ends.

Row 8 (skirt): Attach thread to 11th ch-3 sp of Row 7, work beg shell in same sp; shell in next ch-3 sp; ch 1, turn.

Row 9: Sl st in 2 dc and ch-2 sp, beg d-shell in same sp; d-shell in next shell; ch 1, turn.

Row 10: Sl st in 2 dc and ch-2 sp, beg shell; *ch 2, (shell in next ch-2 sp) twice, ch 2, shell in next ch-2 sp; ch 1, turn.

Row 11: Sl st in 2 dc and ch-2 sp, beg shell; *ch 2, V-st in next ch-2 sp, ch 2, (shell in next shell**) twice; rep from * to **; ch 1, turn.

Row 12: Sl st in 2 dc and ch-2 sp, beg shell; *ch 2, 7 dc in V-st, ch 2, (shell in next shell*) twice; rep from * to *; ch 1, turn.

Row 13: Sl st in 2 dc and ch-2 sp, beg shell; *(ch 1, dc in next dc of 7-dc group) 7 times, ch 1, (shell in next shell*) twice; rep from * to *; ch 1, turn.

Row 14: Sl st in 2 dc and ch-2 sp, beg shell; *ch 3, skip one ch-1 sp, (sc in next ch-1 sp, ch 3) 6 times, (shell in next shell**) twice; rep from * to **, ch 1, turn.

Row 15: Sl st in 2 dc and ch-2 sp, beg shell; *ch 3, skip one ch-3 sp, (sc in next ch-3 sp, ch 3) 5 times**, (d-shell in next shell) twice; rep from * to **, shell in next shell; ch 1, turn.

Row 16: Sl st in 2 dc and ch-2 sp, beg shell; *ch 3, skip one ch-3 sp, (sc in next ch-3 sp, ch 3) 4 times**, (shell in next ch-2 sp) 4 times; rep from * to **, shell in next shell; ch 1, turn.

Row 17: Sl st in 2 dc and ch-2 sp, beg shell; *ch 3, skip one ch-3 sp, (sc in next ch-3 sp, ch 3) 3 times**; (shell in next shell, ch 1) 3 times, shell in next shell; rep from * to **, shell in next shell; ch 1, turn.

Row 18: Sl st in 2 dc and ch-2 sp, beg shell; *ch 3, skip one ch-3 sp, (sc in next ch-3 sp, ch 3) twice; (shell in next shell**, ch 2) 3 times, shell in next shell; rep from * to **; ch 1, turn.

Row 19: Sl st in 2 dc and ch-2 sp, beg shell; *ch 3, skip one ch-3 sp, sc in next ch-3 sp, (ch 3, shell in next shell**) 4 times; rep from * to **; ch 1, turn.

Row 20: Sl st in 2 dc and ch-2 sp, beg shell; (ch 3, shell in next shell) 5 times; ch 1, turn.

Row 21: Sl st in 2 dc and ch-2 sp; (ch 3, dc) in same sp; *in next ch-3 sp work (2 dc, picot, ch 1, 2 dc); in next shell work (2 dc, picot, ch 1, 2 dc); rep from * across to last shell, work 2 dc in last shell. Finish off; weave in thread ends.

Right Arm

Row 1: With right side facing, skip 4 ch-3 sps on Row 7; attach thread to next ch-3 sp, ch 3 and 2 dc in same sp, 3 dc in next ch-3 sp, ch 3, turn.

Row 2: *(YO, insert hook in next st and draw up a lp, YO and draw through 2 lps) twice; YO and draw through rem 3 lps: decrease made; rep from * once more, dc in next dc; ch 3, turn.

Row 3: Dc in next 3 sts, ch 3, turn.

Row 4: (YO, insert hook in next st and draw up a lp, YO and draw through 2 lps) twice, YO and draw through rem 3 lps; dc in next dc, ch 3, turn.

Row 5: Dc in next 2 dc, ch 3, turn.

Row 6: Dc in next 2 sts. Finish off.

Left Arm

Row 1: Attach thread to 16th ch-3 sp of Row 7; 3 dc in next ch-3 sp; ch 3, turn work.

Rows 2 through 6: Work same as for right arm. Finish off; weave in thread ends.

Pineapple Triangles

STITCH GUIDE

Beginning Shell (beg shell): In specified sp, work (ch 3, dc, ch 2, 2 dc).

Shell: In specified st work (2 dc, ch 2, 2 dc).

Beginning Double Shell (beg d-shell): In specified st work [(ch 3, dc, (ch 2, 2 dc) twice].

Double Shell (d-shell): In specified sp work [(2 dc, ch 2) twice, 2 dc].

Picot: Ch 5, sl st in 4th ch from hook.

INSTRUCTIONS

Ch 6; join with a sl st to form a ring.

Rnd 1 (right side): Ch 7 (counts as dc and ch-4), (3 dc in ring, ch 4) 3 times, 2 dc in ring; join with a sl st in 3rd ch of beg ch-7.

Rnd 2: Sl st in ch-4 sp, beg d-shell in same sp; (d-shell in next ch-4 sp) 3 times; join with a sl st in 3rd ch of beg ch-3.

Rnd 3: Sl st in dc and ch-2 sp, beg shell in same sp; ch 5, (shell in next ch-2 sp) twice, ch 3, (shell in next ch-2 sp) twice, ch 5; (shell in next ch-2 sp) twice, ch 3, shell in next ch-2 sp; join with a sl st in 3rd ch of ch-3.

Rnd 4: Sl st in dc and ch-2 sp, beg shell in same sp; *10 dc in ch-5 sp, (shell in next shell) twice; 6 dc in ch-3 sp, (shell in next shell**) twice; rep from * around, ending last rep at **; join with a sl st in 3rd ch of ch-3.

Rnd 5: Sl st in dc and ch-2 sp, beg shell in same sp; (ch 1, dc in next dc of 10-dc group) 10 times, ch 1, (shell in next shell) twice; (ch 1, dc in next dc of 6-dc group) 6 times, ch 1, (shell in next shell**) twice; rep from * around, ending last rep at **; join with a sl st in 3rd ch of ch-3.

Rnd 6: Sl st in dc and ch-2 sp, beg shell in same sp; *ch 3, skip one ch-1 sp, (sc in next ch-1 sp, ch 3) 9 times; (shell in next shell) twice, ch 3, skip one ch-1 sp, (sc in next ch-1 sp, ch 3) 5 times; (shell in next shell**) twice, rep from * around, ending last rep at **; join with a sl st in 3rd ch of ch-3.

Rnd 7: Sl st in dc and ch-2 sp, beg shell; *ch 3, skip one ch-3 sp, (sc in next ch-3 sp, 3 dc in front lp of next sc, sc in next ch-3 sp, ch 3) 4 times; (shell in next shell) twice, ch 3, skip one ch-3 sp; (sc in next ch-3 sp, 3 dc in front lp of next sc, sc in next ch-3 sp, ch 3) twice, (shell in next shell**) twice; rep from * around, ending last rep at **; join with a sl st in 3rd ch of ch-3.

Note: *Remainder of pineapple is worked in rows.*

Row 1: Sl st in dc and ch-2 sp, beg shell in same sp; (ch 3, skip one dc, sc in next dc, ch 3,** sc in ch-3 sp) 4 times, end at ** on last rep, shell in next shell; ch 1, turn.

Row 2: Sl st in 2 dc and ch-2 sp, beg shell; ch 3, skip one ch-3 sp, (sc in next ch-3 sp, 3 dc in back lp of next sc, sc in next ch-3 sp, ch 3) 3 times; shell in next shell; ch 1, turn.

Row 3: Sl st in 2 dc and ch-2 sp, beg shell; ch 3, (skip one dc, sc in next dc, ch 3, sc in ch-3 sp, ch 3) twice; skip one dc, sc in next dc, ch 3, shell in next shell; ch 1, turn.

Row 4: Sl st in 2 dc and ch-2 sp, beg shell; ch 3, skip one ch-3 sp, (sc in next ch-3 sp, 3 dc in back lp of next sc, sc in next ch-3 sp, ch 3) twice, shell in next shell; ch 1, turn.

Row 5: Sl st in 2 dc and ch-2 sp, beg shell; ch 3, skip one dc, sc in next dc, ch 3, sc in ch-3 sp, ch 3; skip one dc, sc in next dc, ch 3, shell in next shell; ch 1, turn.

Row 6: Sl st in 2 dc and ch-2 sp, beg shell; ch 3, skip one ch-3 sp, sc in next ch-3 sp; 3 dc in back lp of next sc, sc in next ch-3 sp, ch 3, shell in next shell; ch 1, turn.

Row 7: Sl st in 2 dc and ch-2 sp, beg shell; ch 3, skip one dc, sc in next dc, ch 3, shell in next shell; ch 1, turn.

Row 8: Sl st in 2 dc and ch-2 sp, beg shell, shell in next shell; ch 1, turn.

Row 9: Sl st in 2 dc and ch-2 sp, ch 3, dc, 2 dc in next shell. Finish off; weave in thread ends.

With right side facing, join thread to shell on right-hand side of next large pineapple.

Work Rows 1 through 9 to complete next large pineapple.

With right side facing, join thread to shell on right hand side of next small pineapple.

Work Rows 5 through 9 to complete two small pineapples.

Do not finish off on last small pineapple.

Edging

Rnd 1: Ch 1, sc in dc; *picot, ch 2**, sc in first dc of next row; rep from * around, ending last rep at ** on last rep; join with a sl st in first sc. Finish off; weave in thread ends.

Circle of Pineapples

STITCH GUIDE

Beginning Shell (beg shell): In specified st work (ch 3 dc, ch 2, 2 dc).

Shell: In specified st work (2 dc, ch 2, 2 dc).

Beginning Double Shell (beg d-shell): In specified st work [ch 3, dc, (ch 2, 2 dc) twice] .

Double Shell (d-shell): In specified st work [(2 dc, ch 2) twice, 2 dc].

V Stitch (V-st): In specified st work (dc, ch 3, dc).

Picot: Ch 3, sl st in dc.

Picot cluster (picot-Cl): In last sc made work (ch 3, sl st, ch 5, sl st, ch 3, sl st).

INSTRUCTIONS

Rnd 1: Ch 7; (dc in first ch, ch 3) 4 times; dc in first ch, ch 1, join with hdc in 4th of beg ch-7.

Rnd 2: Ch 1, sc in join; *ch 3, 4 dc around post (vertical bar) of next dc**, sc in next ch-3 sp; rep from * around, end at ** on last rep; join with a sl st in first sc.

Rnd 3: Sl st in ch-3 sp, beg shell in same sp; *ch 3, shell in next ch-3 sp; rep from * around, ch 3, join with a sl st in 3rd ch of beg ch-3.

Rnd 4: Sl st in dc and ch-2 sp, beg shell in same sp; *ch 3, sc in ch-3 sp, ch 3**, shell in next shell; rep from * around, end at ** on last rep; join with a sl st in 3rd ch of ch-3.

Rnd 5: Sl st in dc and ch-2 sp, beg shell; *(ch 3, sc in ch-3 sp) twice, ch 3**, shell in next shell; rep from * around, end at ** on last rep; join with a sl st in 3rd ch of ch-3.

Rnd 6: Sl st in dc and ch-2 sp, beg shell; *ch 3, skip one ch-3 sp, 6 tr in next ch-3 sp, ch 3**, shell in next shell; rep from * around, end at ** on last rep; join with a sl st in 3rd ch of beg ch-3.

Rnd 7: Sl st in dc and ch-2 sp, beg shell; *ch 2, (tr in tr, ch 1) 5 times, tr in next tr, ch 2**, shell in next shell; rep from * around, end at ** on last rep; join with a sl st in 3rd ch of beg ch-3.

Rnd 8: Sl st in dc and ch-2 sp, beg d-shell; *(ch 3, sc in ch-1 sp) 5 times, ch 3**, d-shell in next shell; rep from * around, end at ** on last rep, join with a sl st in 3rd ch of ch-3.

Rnd 9: Sl st in dc and ch-2 sp, beg shell; ch 3, shell in next ch-2 sp, ch 3, *skip one ch-3 sp, (sc in next ch-3 sp, ch 3) 4 times**, (shell in next ch-2 sp, ch 3) twice; rep from * around, end at ** on last rep, join with a sl st in 3rd ch of ch-3.

Rnd 10: Sl st in dc and ch-2 sp, beg shell; *ch 2, V-st in ch-3 sp, ch 2, shell in next shell, ch 3, *skip one ch-3 sp, (sc in next ch-3 sp, ch 3) 3 times**, shell in shell; rep from * around, end at ** on last rep, join with a sl st in 3rd ch of ch-3.

Rnd 11: Sl st in dc and ch-2 sp, beg shell; *ch 1, in V-st work (V-st, ch 3, V-st), ch 1, shell in next shell, ch 3; *skip one ch-3 sp, (sc in next ch-3 sp, ch 3) twice**, shell in next shell; rep from * around, end at ** on last rep; join with a sl st in 3rd ch of ch-3.

Rnd 12: Sl st in dc and ch-2 sp, beg shell; *ch 11, sc in V-st, ch 5, sc in next V-st, ch 11, shell in next shell, ch 3, *skip one ch-3 sp, sc in next ch-3 sp, ch 3**, shell in next shell; rep from * around, end at ** on last rep; join with a sl st in 3rd ch of ch-3.

Rnd 13: Sl st in dc and ch-2 sp, beg shell; *sc in each of ch-11, in ch-5 sp work, (4 sc, picot-Cl, 3 sc), sc in each of ch-11, (shell in next shell**) twice; rep from * around, end at ** on last rep; join with a sl st in 3rd ch of ch-3.

Rnd 14: Sl st in dc and ch-2 sp, ch 3, dc in shell; *ch 20, sc in free ch-3 sp of Rnd 12 (beneath picot cluster) ch 20, (2 dc in next shell**) twice; rep from * around, end at ** on last rep, join with a sl st in 3rd ch of ch-3.

Rnd 15: Ch 1, sc in join, sc in next dc, picot-Cl, sc in next 2 dc, in ch-20 sp work, *(sc in next 2 chs, ch 2, skip one ch, dc in next ch, picot, dc in next ch, ch 2, skip one ch) 3 times, sc in next 2 chs**, sc in sc, rep from * to * once more**; sc in next 2 dc, picot-Cl, sc in next 2 dc; rep from * around, end at ** on last rep; join with a sl st in first sc. Finish off; weave in thread ends.

Pineapple Ring

STITCH GUIDE

Beginning Shell (beg shell): In specified sp work (ch 3, dc, ch 2, 2 dc).

Shell: In specified st work (2 dc, ch 2, 2 dc).

V-Stitch (V-st): In specified st work (dc, ch 3, dc).

Double V-Stitch (DV-st): In specified st work [(dc, ch 3) twice, dc].

Cluster (Cl): YO, insert hook in specified st, YO and draw up a lp, YO and draw through 2 lps on hook) twice, YO and draw through rem lps on hook.

Picot: Ch 3, sl st in last st made.

INSTRUCTIONS

Rnd 1: Ch 2; 6 sc in first ch; join with a sl st in first sc.

Rnd 2: Ch 1, sc in join; *ch 6, sc in next sc, rep from * around; ch 2, join with a tr in first sc.

Rnd 3: Ch 1; *in next ch-6 sp work (sc, ch 2, cl, ch 5, sl st in cl just made, ch 2, sc), rep from * around; join with a sl st in first sc. Finish off; weave in thread ends.

Rnd 4: Attach thread to any ch-5 sp, ch 1, sc in join; *ch 8, sc in next ch-5 sp; rep from * around, ch 8; join with a sl st in first sc.

Rnd 5: Ch 6 (counts as a dc and ch-3), V-st in join; *in ch-8 sp work (ch 3, sc, picot, sc, ch 3) **, DV-st in next sc; rep from * around, end at ** on last rep; join with a sl st in 3rd ch of beg ch-6.

Rnd 6: Sl st in ch-3 sp, beg shell in same sp; *shell in next ch-3 sp, ch 2, V-st in picot, ch 2 **, shell in next ch-3 sp of DV-st; rep from * around, end at ** on last rep, join with a sl st in 3rd ch of beg ch-3.

Rnd 7: Sl st in dc and ch-2 sp, beg shell in same sp; *ch 3, shell in next shell, ch 2, 6 dc in V-st, ch 2**, shell in next shell; rep from * around, end at ** on last rep; join with a sl st in 3rd ch of ch-3.

Rnd 8: Sl st in dc and ch-2 sp, beg shell in same sp; *ch 2, V-st in ch-3 sp, ch 2, shell in next shell, (ch 1, dc in next dc) 6 times, ch 2 **, shell in next shell; rep from * around, end at ** on last rep; join with a sl st in 3rd ch of ch-3.

Rnd 9: Sl st in dc and ch-2 sp, beg shell; *ch 2, DV-st in V-st, ch 2, shell in next shell, ch 3, skip one ch-3 sp, (sc in next ch-1 sp, ch 3) 5 times**, shell in next shell; rep from * around, end at ** on last rep; join with a sl st in 3rd ch of ch-3.

Rnd 10: Sl st in dc and ch-2 sp, beg shell; *ch 2, V-st in ch-3 sp, ch 3, V-st in next ch-3 sp, ch 2, shell in next shell, ch 3, skip one ch-3 sp, (sc in next ch-3 sp, ch 3) 4 times**, shell in next shell; rep from * around, end at ** on last rep; join with a sl st in 3rd ch of ch-3.

Rnd 11: Sl st in dc and ch-2 sp, beg shell; *(ch 3, dc in next dc) twice, ch 3, dc in next ch-3 sp, (ch 3, dc in next dc) twice, ch 3, shell in next shell, ch 3, skip one ch-3 sp, (sc in next ch-3 sp, ch 3) 3 times**, shell in next shell; rep from * around, end at ** on last rep; join with a sl st in 3rd ch of ch-3.

Rnd 12: Sl st in dc and ch-2 sp, beg shell; *(ch 4, dc in next dc) twice, ch 4, V-st in next dc, (ch 4, dc in next dc) twice; ch 4, shell in next shell, ch 3, skip one ch-3 sp, (sc in next ch-3 sp, ch 3) twice**, shell in next shell; rep from * around, end at ** on last rep; join with a sl st in 3rd ch of ch-3.

Rnd 13: Sl st in dc and ch-2 sp, beg shell; *(ch 5, dc in next dc) 6 times, ch 5, shell in next shell, ch 3, skip one ch-3 sp, sc in next ch-3 sp, ch 3**, shell in next shell; rep from * around, end at ** on last rep; join with a sl st in 3rd ch of ch-3.

Rnd 14: Sl st in dc and ch-2 sp, ch 2, dc; *[in next ch-5 sp work (Cl, ch 3) twice, Cl)] 7 times; Cl in next shell, picot**, Cl in next shell; rep from * around, end at ** on last rep; join with a sl st in first dc. Finish off; weave in thread ends.

Marching Pineapples

STITCH GUIDE

Beginning Shell (beg shell): In specified sp work (ch 3, dc, ch 2, 2 dc).

Shell: In specified st work (2 dc, ch 2, 2 dc).

Beginning Double Shell (beg d-shell): In specified st work [ch 3, dc, (ch 2, 2 dc) twice].

Double shell (d-shell): In specified st work [(2 dc, ch 2) twice, 2 dc].

V Stitch (V-st): In specified st work (dc, ch 2, dc).

Picot: Ch 3, sl st in last st made.

Cluster (CL): (YO, insert hook in specified st, YO and draw up a lp, YO and draw through 2 lps on hook) twice, YO and draw through rem 3 lps on hook.

INSTRUCTIONS

Rnd 1: Ch 4; join with a sl st in first ch to form a ring; ch 1, (sc in ring, ch 3) 5 times, ch 1, join with a hdc in first sc.

Rnd 2: Ch 1, sc in join, *ch 4, sc in next ch-3 sp; rep from * around, ch 2, join with a hdc in first sc.

Rnd 3: Ch 1, sc in join; *ch 5, sc in next ch-4 sp; rep from * around, ch 2, dc in first sc.

Rnd 4: Ch 1, sc in join; *ch 8, sc in next ch-5 sp; rep from * around, ch 4, tr in first sc.

Rnd 5: Ch 3, 3 dc, hdc, 2 sc in same sp as join; *in next ch-8 sp work (2 sc, hdc, 7 dc, hdc, 2 sc), rep from * around, in next sp work (2 sc, hdc, 3 dc); join with a sl st in 3rd ch of ch-3.

Rnd 6: Ch 5, (count as dc and ch-2), dc in same sp as join; *ch 2, skip one dc, sc in next dc, ch 6, skip 8 sts, sc in next st, ch 2**; skip one dc, V-st in next dc; rep from * around, end at ** on last rep; join with a sl st in 3rd ch of beg ch-5.

Rnd 7: Sl st in ch-2 sp, beg shell; *in ch-6 sp work (ch 1, Cl) 7 times; ch 1**, shell in V-st; rep from * around, end at ** on last rep; join with a sl st in 3rd ch of ch-3.

Rnd 8: Sl st in dc and ch-2 sp, beg d-shell in same sp; *ch 3, skip one ch-1 sp, (sc in next ch-1 sp, ch 3) 6 times**, d-shell in next shell; rep from * around, end at ** on last rep; join with a sl st in 3rd ch of ch-3.

Rnd 9: Sl st in dc and ch-2 sp, beg shell; *shell in next ch-2 sp, ch 3, skip one ch-3 sp, (sc in next ch-3 sp, ch 3) 5 times**, shell in next ch-2 sp; rep from * around, end at ** on last rep; join with a sl st in 3rd of ch-3.

Rnd 10: Sl st in dc and ch-2 sp, beg shell; *ch 3, shell in next shell, ch 3, skip one ch-3 sp, (sc in next ch-3 sp, ch 3) 4 times**, shell in next shell; rep from * around, end at ** on last rep; join with a sl st in 3rd ch of ch-3.

Rnd 11: Sl st in dc and ch-2 sp, beg shell; *in ch-3 sp work (ch 3, sc, picot, sc, ch 3); shell in next shell, ch 3; skip one ch-3 sp, (sc in next ch-3 sp, ch 3) 3 times**, shell in next shell; rep from * around, end at ** on last rep; join with a sl st in 3rd ch of ch-3.

Rnd 12: Sl st in dc and ch-2 sp, beg shell; *ch 11, shell in next shell, ch 3, skip one ch-3 sp, (sc in next ch-3 sp, ch 3) twice**, shell in next shell; rep from * around, end at ** on last rep, join with a sl st in 3rd of ch-3.

Rnd 13: Sl st in dc and ch-2 sp, beg shell; *ch 3, skip 2 ch sts, (sc in next two ch sts, picot) 3 times, sc in next ch st, ch 3, shell in next shell, ch 5, skip one ch-3 sp, sc in next ch-3 sp, ch 5 **, shell in next shell; rep from * around, end at ** on last rep, join with a sl st in 3rd of ch-3.

Rnd 14: Sl st in dc and ch-2 sp, ch 1, sc; *ch 13, skip one picot, sc in next picot, (ch 13, sc in shell) ** twice; rep from * around, end at ** on last rep; ch 11, join with hdc in first sc.

Rnd 15: Ch 1, sc in join; *V-st in sc, skip two chs, (sc in next 3 chs, picot) twice **; sc in next 3 chs; rep from * around, end at ** on last rep; sc in next 2 sts; join with a sl st in first sc. Finish off; weave in thread ends.

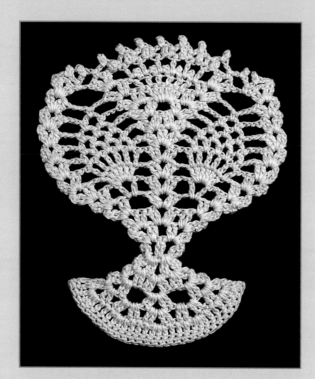

Pineapple Vase

STITCH GUIDE

Beginning Shell (beg shell): In specified sp work (ch 3, dc, ch 2, 2 dc).

Shell: In specified st work (2 dc, ch 2, 2 dc).

Double Shell (d-shell): In specified st work [(2 dc, ch 2) twice, 2 dc].

Picot: Ch 3, sl st in last st made.

Large Picot: Ch 5, sl st in 4th ch from hook.

V-Stitch (V-st): In specified st work (dc, ch 2, dc).

INSTRUCTIONS

Ch 8.

Row 1: Dc in 4th ch from hook; (ch 2, dc in each of next two chs) twice; ch 1, turn.

Row 2: Sl st in 2 dc and ch-2 sp, beg shell in same sp; ch 2, shell in next ch-2 sp; ch 1, turn.

Row 3: Sl st in 2 dc and ch-2 sp, beg shell in same sp; (shell in next ch-2 sp) twice; ch 1, turn.

Row 4: Sl st in 2 dc and ch-2 sp, beg shell; (ch 3, shell in next shell) twice; ch 1, turn.

Row 5: Sl st in 2 dc and ch-2 sp, beg shell; (ch 2, V-st in ch-2 sp, ch 2, shell in next shell) twice; ch 1, turn.

Row 6: Sl st in 2 dc and ch-2 sp, beg shell; (ch 2, 6 dc in V-st, ch 2, shell in next shell) twice; ch 1, turn.

Row 7: Sl st in 2 dc and ch-2 sp, beg shell; [ch 1, (dc in dc, ch 1) 6 times, shell in next shell] twice; ch 1, turn.

Row 8: Sl st in 2 dc and ch-2 sp, beg shell; *ch 3, skip one ch-1 sp, (sc in next ch-1 sp, ch 3) 5 times**, d-shell in next shell, rep from * to **, shell in next shell; ch 1, turn.

Row 9: Sl st in 2 dc and ch-2 sp, beg shell; *ch 3, skip one ch-3 sp; (sc in next ch-3 sp, ch 3) 4 times*, (shell in next ch-2 sp*) twice, rep from * to *; shell in next shell, ch 1, turn.

Row 10: Sl st in 2 dc and ch-2 sp, beg shell; *ch 3, skip one ch-3 sp, (sc in next ch-3 sp, ch 3) 3 times, shell in next shell**, ch 2, shell in next shell, rep from * to **; ch 1, turn.

Row 11: Sl st in 2 dc and ch-2 sp, beg shell; *ch 3, skip one ch-3 sp, (sc in next ch-3 sp, ch 3) twice, shell in next shell**; 6 dc in ch-2 sp, shell in next shell, rep from * to **; ch 1, turn.

Row 12: Sl st in 2 dc and ch-2 sp, beg shell; *ch 3, skip one ch-3 sp, sc in next ch-3 sp, ch 3, shell in next shell**; (dc in dc, picot) 5 times, dc in next dc, shell in next shell, rep from * to **; ch 1, turn.

Row 13: Sl st in 2 dc and ch-2 sp, beg shell; ch 2, shell in next shell, (ch 4, sl st in first ch, ch 1, dc in next dc) 6 times, ch 4, sl st in first ch, shell in next shell, ch 2, shell in next shell; ch 1, turn work.

Row 14: Sc in dc, large picot, ch 2, sc in ch-2 sp, large picot, ch 2, sc in shell, (large picot, ch 2, sc in next dc) 6 times; large picot, ch 2, sc in shell, large picot, ch 2, sc in ch-2 sp, large picot, ch 2, sc in last dc of shell.

Base

Rotate pieces with beginning ch-8 at top. Attach yarn with sl st in first sp between pairs of dc.

Row 1: Beg shell in first sp, ch 2, shell in next sp; ch 1, turn.

Row 2: Sl st in 2 dc and ch-2 sp, beg shell, (ch 2 shell in next ch-2 sp) twice; ch 1, turn.

Row 3: Sl st in 2 dc and ch-2 sp, beg shell (ch 3, shell in next shell) twice; ch 1, turn.

Row 4: Sl st in 2 dc and ch-2 sp, beg shell, (shell in next ch-3 sp, shell in next shell) twice; ch 3, turn.

Row 5: Skip first dc of first shell, dc in next dc (2 dc in ch-2 sp, dc in next 4 dc) 4 times, 2 dc in next sp, dc in last 2 dc.

Finish off; weave in thread ends.

Pineapple Clusters

STITCH GUIDE

Beginning Shell (beg shell): In specified sp work (ch 3, dc, ch 2, 2 dc).

Shell: In specified st work (2 dc, ch 2, 2 dc).

Beginning Double Shell (beg d-shell): In specified st work [ch 3, dc, (ch 2, 2 dc) twice].

Double shell (d-shell): In specified st work [(2 dc, ch 2) twice, 2 dc].

Cluster (Cl): YO, insert hook in specified st, YO and draw up a lp, YO and draw through 2 lps on hook) twice, YO and draw through rem lps on hook.

V Stitch (V-st): In specified st work (dc, ch 2, dc).

Picot: Ch 3, sl st in last st made before ch-3.

Picot cluster (picot-Cl): In last st made work (ch 3, sl st, ch 5, sl st, ch 3, sl st).

INSTRUCTIONS

Ch 6; join with a sl st to form ring.

Rnd 1: Ch 1, 12 sc in ring; join with a sl st in first sc.

Rnd 2: Ch 7, (counts as dc and ch-4); *skip one sc, dc in next sc, ch 4; rep from * around, ch 2; join with hdc in 3rd ch of beg ch-7.

Rnd 3: Ch 1, sc in join; *ch 6, sc in next ch-4 sp; rep from * around, ch 2; join with a tr in first sc.

Rnd 4: Work beg shell; *ch 5, shell in next ch-6 sp; rep from * around, ch 5; join with a sl st in 3rd ch of ch-3.

Rnd 5: Sl st in dc and ch-2 sp, beg d-shell in same sp; *ch 3, sc in ch-5 sp, ch 3**, d-shell in next shell; rep from * around, end at ** on last rep; join with a sl st in 3rd ch of ch-3.

Rnd 6: Sl st in dc and ch-2 sp, beg shell in same sp; *shell in next ch-2 sp, ch 7**, shell in next ch-2 sp; rep from * around, end at ** on last rep; join with a sl st in 3rd ch of ch-3.

Rnd 7: Sl st in dc and ch-2 sp, beg shell; *ch 5, shell in next shell, ch 7**, shell in next shell; rep from * around, end at ** on last rep; join with a sl st in 3rd ch of ch-3.

Rnd 8: Sl st in dc and ch-2 sp, beg shell; *ch 2, in ch-5 sp work (5 dc, ch 3, 5 dc), ch 2, shell in next shell, ch 4, sc over both ch-7 sps of Rnd 6 and 7, ch 4**, shell in next shell; rep from * around, end at ** on last rep; join with a sl st in 3rd ch of ch-3.

Rnd 9: Sl st in dc and ch-2 sp, beg shell; *(ch 1, dc in next dc of next 5-dc group) 5 times, ch 1, dc in ch-3 sp; (ch 1, dc in next dc of next 5-dc group) 5 times, ch 1, shell in next shell, ch 1; (dc in next ch-4 sp) twice, ch 1**, shell in next shell; rep from * around, end at ** on last rep; join with a sl st in 3rd ch of ch-3.

Rnd 10: Sl st in dc and ch-2 sp, ch 1, sc in center sp of shell, *ch 3, skip one ch-1 sp; (sc in next ch-1 sp, ch 3) 4 times, skip one dc, V-st in next dc; ch 3, skip one ch-1 sp, (sc in next ch-1 sp, ch 3) 4 times, sc in center sp of next shell, ch 5**, sc in center sp of next shell; rep from * around, end at ** on last rep; ch 1, tr in first sc.

Rnd 11: Work beg d-shell; *ch 3, skip one ch-3 sp, (sc in next ch-3 sp, ch 3) 3 times; d-shell in V-st, ch 3, skip one ch-3 sp; (sc in next ch-3 sp, ch 3) 3 times**, d-shell in ch-5 sp; rep from * around, end at ** on last rep; join with a sl st in 3rd ch of ch-3.

Rnd 12: Sl st in dc and ch-2 sp, beg shell; *ch 3, shell in next ch-2 sp, ch 3, skip one ch-3 sp, (sc in next ch-3 sp, ch 3) twice**; shell in ch-2 sp; rep from * around, end at ** on last rep; join with a sl st in 3rd ch of ch-3.

Rnd 13: Sl st in dc and ch-2 sp, beg shell; *ch 7, shell in next shell, ch 3, skip one ch-3 sp, sc in next ch-3 sp; ch 3**, shell in next shell; rep from * around, end at ** on last rep, join with a sl st in 3rd ch of ch-3.

Rnd 14: Sl st in dc and ch-2 sp, beg shell; *ch 6, skip ch-7 sp of Rnd 13 working in front of ch-7, sc in ch-3 sp of Rnd 12; ch 6, shell in next shell**, ch 3, shell in next shell; rep from * around, end at ** on last rep, ch 1, join with hdc in 3rd ch of ch-3.

Rnd 15: (Ch 2, dc, picot) in join; *Cl in next shell, ch 5, in next ch-6 sp work (sc, picot Cl, sc), ch 3; sc in ch-7 sp of Rnd 13, ch 3, in ch-6 sp work (sc, picot-Cl, sc); ch 5, Cl in shell, picot,** Cl in ch-3 sp, picot, Cl in next shell; ch 5, in next ch-6 sp of Rnd 14 work (sc, picot, sc), ch 5, (tr, picot-Cl, tr) in ch-7 sp of Rnd 13; ch 5 in next ch-6 sp of Rnd 14 work (sc, picot, sc); ch 5, Cl in next shell, picot** Cl and picot in ch-3 sp; rep from * around, end at ** on last rep, sl st in first dc. Finish off; weave in thread ends.

Mystical Pineapples

STITCH GUIDE

Beginning Shell (beg shell): In specified st work (ch 3 dc, ch 2, 2 dc).

Shell: In specified st work (2 dc, ch 2, 2 dc).

Beginning Double Shell (beg d-shell): In specified st work [ch 3, dc, (ch 2, 2 dc) twice].

Double Shell (d-shell): In specified st work [(2 dc, ch 2) twice, 2 dc].

V Stitch (V-st): In specified st work (dc, ch 3, dc).

Picot: Ch 3, sl st in last st made.

INSTRUCTIONS

Ch 6; join with a sl st to form a ring.

Rnd 1: Ch 6 (count as a dc and ch-3), (dc in ring, ch 3) 4 times, dc in ring, ch 1; join with hdc in 3rd ch of beg ch-6.

Rnd 2: Ch 1, sc in join; *ch 3, 6 dc around post (vertical bar) of next dc**, sc in next ch-3 sp; rep from * around, end at ** on last rep; join with a sl st in first sc.

Rnd 3: Ch 1, sc in join; *ch 4, sc in next sc; rep from * around, ch 4; join with a sl st in first sc.

Rnd 4: Sl st in ch-4 sp, beg d-shell in same sp; *ch 2, V-st in next ch-4 sp, ch 2**, d-shell in next ch-4 sp; rep from * around, end at ** on last rep; join with a sl st in 3rd ch of beg ch-3.

Rnd 5: Sl st in dc and ch-2 sp, beg shell in same sp; *ch 3, shell in next ch-2 sp, ch 2, 8 dc in V-st, ch 2**, shell in next ch-2 sp; rep from * around, end at ** on last rep, join with a sl st in 3rd ch of ch-3.

Rnd 6: Sl st in dc and ch-2 sp, beg shell in same sp; *ch 2, dc in ch-3 sp, ch 2, shell in next shell, (ch 1, dc in dc) 8 times; ch 1**, shell in next shell; rep from * around; end at ** on last rep; join with a sl st in 3rd of ch-3.

Rnd 7: Sl st in dc and ch-2 sp, beg shell; *ch 2, V-st in dc, ch 2, shell in next shell, ch 3, skip one ch-1 sp, (sc in next ch-1 sp, ch 3) 7 times**, shell in next shell; rep from * end at ** on last repeat, join with a sl st in 3rd ch of ch-3.

Rnd 8: Sl st in dc and ch-2 sp, beg shell in same sp; *ch 2, d-shell in V-st, ch 2, shell in next shell, ch 3, skip one ch-3 sp, (sc in next ch-3 sp, ch 3) 6 times**; shell in next shell; rep from * end at ** on last rep; join with a sl st in 3rd ch of ch-3.

Rnd 9: Sl st in dc and ch-2 sp, beg shell in same sp; *ch 2, (shell in ch-2 sp, ch 2) twice, shell in next shell, ch 3, skip one ch-3 sp, (sc in next ch-3 sp, ch 3) 5 times**; shell in next shell; rep from * around, end at ** on last rep; join with a sl st in 3rd ch of ch-3.

Rnd 10: Sl st in dc and ch-2 sp, beg shell; *ch 5, shell in next shell, ch 3, shell in next shell; ch 5, shell in next shell, ch 3, skip one ch-3 sp, (sc in next ch-3 sp, ch 3) 4 times**; shell in next shell; rep from * end around, end at ** on last rep; join with a sl st in 3rd ch of ch-3.

Rnd 11: Sl st in dc and ch-2 sp, beg shell; *ch 7, shell in next shell, ch 5, shell in next shell, ch 7, shell in next shell; ch 5, skip one ch-3 sp, (sc in next ch-3 sp, ch 3) twice, sc in next ch-3 sp, ch 5**, shell in next shell; rep from * around, end at ** on last rep; join with a sl st in 3rd ch of ch-3.

Rnd 12: Sl st in dc and ch-2 sp, beg shell; *ch 9, shell in next shell, ch 5, shell in next shell, ch 9, shell in next shell; ch 5, skip one ch-5 sp, sc in next ch-3 sp, ch 3, sc in next ch-3 sp, ch 5**, shell in next shell; rep from * around, end at ** on last repeat, join with a sl st in 3rd of ch-3.

Rnd 13: Sl st in dc and ch-2 sp, beg shell; *ch 11, shell in next shell, ch 2, 12 dc in ch-5 sp, ch 2, shell in next shell, ch 11, shell in next shell, ch 5, skip one ch-3 sp, sc in next ch-3 sp, ch 5**, shell in next shell; rep from * end at ** on last repeat, join with a sl st in 3rd of ch-3.

Rnd 14: Sl st in dc and ch-2 sp, beg shell; *ch 13, reach with hook under the top 3 chains to work an sc over 3 lower chains of Rnds 8, 9 and 10 drawing them together; keeping hook under the top 3 chains, ch 13; now continuing on Rnd 14, shell in next shell*; (ch 1, dc in dc) 12 times, ch 1, shell in next shell; rep from * to * once more**, ch 10, shell in next shell; rep from * around, end at ** on last rep; ch 8, join with hdc in 3rd ch of ch-3.

Rnd 15: Ch 1, sc in join; in shell work (2 dc, picot, 2 dc); *ch 1, dc in ch-13 sp, ch 8; over chs of Rnds 11, 12 and 13 work (sc, picot sc), ch 8, dc in next ch-13 sp, ch 1; in next shell work (2 dc, picot, 2 dc)**, ch 1, skip one ch-1 sp; (sc, picot in next ch-1 sp) 10 times, sc in next ch-1 sp, ch 1, in next shell work (2 dc, picot, 2 dc); rep from * to ** once more; in ch 10 sp work [(sc, picot) 5 times***, sc], in next shell work, (2 dc, picot, 2 dc); rep from * around, end at *** on last rep; join with a sl st in first sc. Finish off; weave in ends.

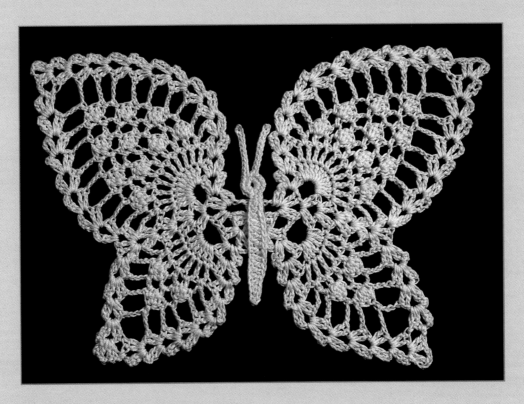

Pineapple Butterfly

STITCH GUIDE

Beginning Shell (beg shell): In specified sp work (ch 3, dc, ch 2, 2 dc) in specified sp.

Shell: In specified st work (2 dc, ch 2, 2 dc).

Beginning Double Shell (beg d-shell: In specified st work [ch 3, dc, (ch 2, 2 dc) twice].

Double shell (d-shell): In specified st work [(2 dc, ch 2) twice, 2 dc].

INSTRUCTIONS

First Half of Butterfly

Ch 6; join with a sl st in to form ring.

Rnd 1: Ch 3, 2 dc in ring, (ch 2, 3 dc in ring) twice, ch 5, 3 dc in ring, ch 1, join with a tr in 3rd ch of beg ch-3.

Note: *Remainder of pattern is worked in rows.*

Row 1: Beg d-shell in same sp as join, shell in next ch-2 sp; ch 1, turn.

Row 2: Sl st in 2 dc and ch-2 sp, beg shell in same sp; *(ch 2, shell in next ch-2 sp) twice; ch 1, turn.

Row 3: Sl st in 2 dc and ch-2 sp; beg shell in same sp; 10 dc in ch-2 sp, shell in next shell, 6 dc in next ch-2 sp, shell in next shell; ch 1, turn.

Row 4: Sl st in 2 dc and ch-2 sp, beg shell; skip 2 dc of shell, (dc in next dc, ch 1) 5 times, dc in next dc, shell in next shell; skip 2 dc of next shell, (dc in next dc, ch 1) 9 times, dc in next dc, shell in next shell; ch 1, turn.

Row 5: Sl st in 2 dc and ch-2 sp, beg shell; (ch 3, sc in ch-1 sp) 9 times, ch 3, shell in next shell; (ch 3, sc in next ch-1 sp) 5 times, ch 3, shell in next shell; ch 1, turn.

Row 6: Sl st in 2 dc and ch-2 sp, beg shell; ch 3, skip one ch-3 sp (sc in ch-3 sp, 3 dc in sc, sc in next ch-3 sp, ch 3) twice; d-shell in next shell, ch 3, skip one ch-3 sp, (sc in next ch-3 sp, 3 dc in sc, sc in next ch-3 sp, ch 3) 4 times, shell in next shell; ch 1, turn.

Row 7: Sl st in 2 dc and ch-2 sp, beg shell; ch 3, (sc in 2nd dc of next 3-dc group, ch 3, sc in ch-3 sp, ch 3) 3 times, sc in 2nd dc, ch 3, shell in next shell; ch 1, turn.

Row 8: Continuing on upper wing sts only, sl st in 2 dc and ch-2 sp, beg shell; ch 3, skip one ch-3 sp, (sc in ch-3 sp, 3 dc in next sc, sc in next ch-3 sp, ch 3) 3 times, shell in next shell; ch 1, turn.

Row 9: Sl st in 2 dc and ch-2 sp, beg shell; ch 3, (sc in 2nd dc of 3-dc group, ch 3, sc in ch-3 sp, ch 3) twice, sc in 2nd dc, ch 3, shell in next shell; ch 1, turn.

Row 10: Sl st in 2 dc and ch-2 sp, beg shell; ch 3, skip one ch-3 sp, (sc in next ch-3 sp, 3 dc in sc, sc in next ch-3 sp, ch 3) twice, shell in next shell; ch 1, turn.

Row 11: Sl st in 2 dc and ch-2 sp, beg shell; ch 3, sc in 2nd dc of 3-dc group, ch 3, sc in ch-3 sp, ch 3, sc in 2nd dc, ch 3, shell in next shell; ch 1, turn.

Row 12: Sl st in 2 dc and ch-2 sp, beg shell; ch 3, skip one ch-3 sp, sc in next ch-3 sp, 3 dc in sc, sc in next ch-3 sp, ch 3, shell in next shell; ch 1, turn.

Row 13: Sl st in 2 dc and ch-2 sp, beg shell; ch 3, sc in 2nd dc of 3-dc group, ch 3, shell in next shell; ch 1, turn.

Rnd 14: Sl st in 2 dc and ch-2 sp, beg shell; shell in next shell, ch 1, turn.

Row 15: Sl st in 2 dc and ch-2 sp, beg shell; sc in next shell. Finish off; weave in thread ends.

Attach thread to free ch-2 sp of d-shell, rep Rows 11 through 15.

Second Half of Butterfly

Row 1: Attach thread to next ch-2 sp, beg shell; ch 2, d-shell in ch-5 sp, ch 1, turn.

Row 2: Sl st in 2 dc and ch-2 sp, beg shell; ch 2, shell in next ch-2 sp, ch 2, shell in next shell; ch 1, turn.

Row 3: Sl st in 2 dc and ch-2 sp, beg shell; 6 dc in ch-2 sp, shell in next shell, 10 dc in next ch-2 sp, shell in next shell; ch 1, turn.

Row 4: Sl st in 2 dc and ch-2 sp, beg shell; skip 2 dc of shell, (dc in next dc, ch 1) 9 times, dc in next dc, shell in next shell, skip 2 dc of next shell, (dc in next dc, ch 1) 5 times, dc in next dc, shell in next shell; ch 1, turn.

Row 5: Sl st in 2 dc and ch-2 sp, beg shell; (ch 3, sc in ch-1 sp) 5 times, ch 3, shell in next shell, (ch 3, sc in next ch-1 sp) 9 times, ch 3, shell in next shell; ch 1, turn.

Row 6: Sl st in 2 dc and ch-2 sp, beg shell; ch 3, skip one ch-3 sp, (sc in ch-3 sp, 3 dc in sc, sc in next ch-3 sp, ch 3) 4 times; d-shell in next shell, ch 3, skip one ch-3 sp, (sc in next ch-3 sp, 3 dc in sc, sc in next ch-3 sp, ch 3) twice, shell in next shell; ch 1, turn.

Repeat Rows 11 to 15 of First Half of Butterfly.

Attach thread to ch-2 sp of d-shell, rep Rows 7 through 15 of First Half of Butterfly.

Body

Ch 20.

Row 1: Sc in 2nd ch from hook, sc in next ch , hdc in next 2 chs, dc in next 4 chs, tr in next 2 chs; dc in next 4 chs, hdc in next 2 chs, sc in next 2 chs, 6 sc in first ch; *ch 10, sl st in 2nd ch from hook and in next 8 chs, sl st in last sc made;* 2 sc in first ch, rep from * to * once more; 6 sc in first ch, sl st in base of next sc. Finish off; weave in thread ends. Sew body to butterfly center.

Fancy Pineapples

STITCH GUIDE

Beginning Shell (beg shell): In specified st work (ch 3, dc, ch 2, 2 dc.

Shell: In specified st work (2 dc, ch 2, 2 dc).

Double Shell (d-shell): In specified sp work (2 dc, ch 2) twice, 2 dc in same st.

V Stitch (V-st): In specified st work (dc, ch 3, dc).

Picot: Ch 3, sl st in last st made.

Beginning Dc and Picot (beg dc and picot): Ch 6, sl st in 4th ch from hook.

INSTRUCTIONS

Ch 6, join with a sl st to form a ring.

Rnd 1: Ch 1, (2 sc in ring, ch 6) 5 times; 2 sc in ring, ch 2; join with a tr in first sc.

Rnd 2: Ch 1, 2 sc in same sp as join; *ch 6, 2 sc in next ch-6 sp; rep from * around; ch 2, join with a tr in first sc.

Rnd 3: Ch 1, in same sp as join work (2 sc, ch 5, sc, ch 5); *in next ch-6 sp work (sc, ch 5, 2 sc, ch 5, sc, ch 5); rep from * around; sc in next ch sp, ch 5, join with a sl st in first sc.

Rnd 4: Ch 1, sc in join, sc in next sc; *ch 4, skip one ch-5 sp, shell in next ch-5 sp**, ch 4; skip one ch-5 sp (sc in next sc) twice; rep from * around, end at **on last rep; ch 2, join with hdc in first sc.

Rnd 5: Ch 6, dc in join, V-st in next ch-4 sp; *ch 2, d-shell in shell, ch 2**, (V-st in next ch-4 sp) twice; rep from * around, end at ** on last rep; join with a sl st in 3rd ch of beg ch-6.

Rnd 6: Sl st in 2 ch sts, beg dc and picot, dc in next V-st; *ch 3, skip one ch-2 sp, shell in next ch-2 sp, ch 3, shell in next ch-2 sp, ch 3**, dc, picot in V-st, dc in next V-st; rep from * around, end at **on last rep, ch 1, hdc in same ch st as first sl st of picot.

Rnd 7: Beg dc and picot, dc in next ch-3 sp; *ch 3, shell in shell, ch 2, V-st in ch-3 sp, ch 2, shell in next shell**; ch 3, (dc, picot in ch-3 sp), dc in next ch-3 sp; rep from * around, end at ** on last rep; ch 1, join with hdc in same ch as first sl st.

Rnd 8: Beg dc and picot, dc in next ch-3 sp; *ch 4, shell in shell, ch 2, 6 dc in V-st, ch 2, shell in next shell**; ch 4, (dc, picot in ch-3 sp), dc in next ch-3 sp; rep from * around, end at ** on last rep; ch 2, join with hdc in same ch as first sl st.

Rnd 9: Beg dc and picot, dc in next ch-4 sp; *ch 4, shell in shell, (ch 1, dc in dc) 6 times, ch 1, shell in next shell**; ch 4, (dc, picot) in ch-4 sp, dc in next ch-4 sp; rep from * around, end at ** on last rep; ch 2, join with hdc in same ch as first sl st.

Rnd 10: Beg dc and picot, dc in next ch-4 sp; *ch 5, shell in shell, ch 3, skip one ch-1 sp (sc in next ch-1 sp, ch 3) 5 times, shell in next shell**; ch 5, (dc, picot) in ch-4 sp, dc in next ch-4 sp; rep from * around, end at ** on last rep; ch 3, join with hdc in same ch as first sl st.

Rnd 11: Beg dc and picot, dc in next ch-5 sp; *ch 5, shell in shell, ch 3, skip one ch-3 sp (sc in next ch-3 sp, ch 3) 4 times, shell in next shell**, ch 5, dc, picot in ch-5 sp, dc in next ch-5 sp; rep from * around, end at ** on last rep, ch 3, join with an hdc in same ch st as first sl st.

Rnd 12: Beg dc and picot, dc in next ch-5 sp; *ch 6, shell in shell, ch 3, skip one ch-3 sp (sc in next ch-3 sp, ch 3) 3 times, shell in next shell**, ch 6, dc, picot in ch-5 sp, dc in next ch-5 sp; rep from * around, end at ** on last rep, ch 4, join with an hdc in same ch st as first sl st.

Rnd 13: Beg dc and picot, dc in next ch-6 sp; *ch 7, shell in shell, ch 3, skip one ch-3 sp (sc in next ch-3 sp, ch 3) twice, shell in next shell**; ch 7, (dc, picot) in ch-6 sp, dc in next ch-6 sp; rep from * around, end at ** on last rep; ch 5, join with hdc in same ch as first sl st.

Rnd 14: Beg dc and picot; *in ch-7 sp work, (dc, ch 5, dc, picot, dc), ch 5, shell in shell, ch 3, skip one ch-3 sp, sc in next ch-3 sp; ch 3, shell in next shell, ch 5, in ch-7 sp work, (dc, picot, dc**, ch 5, dc, picot); rep from * around, end at ** on last rep; ch 2, join with a dc in same ch st as first sl st.

Rnd 15: Beg dc and picot, dc in next ch-5 sp; *ch 7, sc in picot, ch 7, shell in shell, ch 3, shell in next shell; ch 7, sc in picot**, ch 7, dc, picot in ch-5 sp; rep from * around, end at ** on last rep, ch 5, join with hdc in same ch as first sl st.

Rnd 16: Beg dc and picot; in ch-7 sp work (dc, ch 3, sc, picot, sc, ch 3, dc, picot) twice; *dc in shell, ch 3, in ch-3 sp work (sc, picot, sc); ch 3, (dc, picot) in shell; in ch-7 sp work, (dc, ch 3, sc, picot, sc, ch 3, dc, picot**) 4 times; rep from * around, end at ** on last rep; in next sp work (dc, ch 3, sc, picot, sc, ch 3); join with a sl st in same ch as first sl st. Finish off; weave in ends.

Posies and Pineapples

STITCH GUIDE

Beginning Shell (beg shell): In specified sp work (ch 3, dc, ch 2, 2 dc).

Shell: In specified st work (2 dc, ch 2, 2 dc).

V-Stitch (V-st): In specified st work (dc, ch 3, dc).

Picot: Ch 3, sl st in last st made.

Back Post Single Crochet (bp sc): Insert hook from back to front to back around post (vertical bar) of st in row below and draw up a lp; YO and draw through both lps on hook.

Double Triple Crochet (dtr): YO 3 times; insert hook in specified st and draw up a lp; (YO and draw through 2 lps on hook) 4 times, YO and draw through rem lps on hook.

Triple Triple Crochet (ttr): YO 4 times; insert hook in specified st and draw up a lp; (YO and draw through 2 lps on hook) 5 times; YO and draw through rem lps on hook.

INSTRUCTIONS

Motif Center

Ch 6; join with a sl st to form a ring.

Rnd 1: Ch 1; *(2 sc in ring, ch 6) 7 times; 2 sc in ring, ch 3; join with dc in first sc.

Rnds 2 and 3: Ch 1, (sc, picot, sc) in same sp as join; *ch 6, in next ch-6 sp work (sc, picot, sc); rep from * around, ch 3, join with a dc in first sc.

Rnd 4: Ch 1; (sc, picot, sc) in same sp as join; *ch 8, in next ch-6 sp work (sc, picot, sc); rep from * around, ch 3, join with a dtr in first sc.

Rnd 5: (Ch 1, sc, picot, sc) in same sp as join; *ch 10, in next ch-8 sp work (sc, picot, sc); rep from * around, ch 3, join with a ttr in first sc. Do not finish off. Set piece aside.

First Flower

With new thread, ch 4, join with a sl st to form a ring.

Rnd 1: Ch 1, 12 sc in ring; join with a sl st in first sc.

Rnd 2: Ch 1, sc in join; *ch 3, skip one sc, sc in next sc, rep from * around, ch 3, join with a sl st in first sc.

Rnd 3: Sl st in ch-3 sp; *(in ch-3 sp work; sc, ch 2, 2 dc, ch 2, sc) 5 times, in next ch-3 sp work, sc, ch 2, dc, sl st in any picot on Motif Center; finish petal with (dc, ch 2, sc); join with a sl st in first sc. Finish off; weave in thread ends.

Make and join 7 more flowers same as First Flower. **Note:** *Sixth petal of each flower is joined to center unit.*

Continue working on Center Motif and flowers as follows:

Rnd 6: On any flower, attach thread to 2nd sc of Rnd 2 (at end of first petal) with a bp sc; *ch 8, keeping ch-8 behind work, attach ch-8 to opposite edge of flower with a bp sc in first sc of 5th petal; ch 6 in ch-10 sp of center unit work (sc, picot, sc), ch 6** bp sc in 2nd sc of Rnd 2 on next flower; rep from * around, end at ** on last rep; join with a sl st in first bp sc.

First Pineapple

Row 1: Sl st in any ch-8 sp behind flower; in same sp work (beg shell, ch 3, V-st; ch 3, shell); ch 1, turn.

Row 2: Sl st in 2 dc and ch-2 sp, beg shell, ch 2, 8 dc in V-st, ch 2, shell in next shell; ch 1, turn.

Row 3: Sl st in 2 dc and ch-2 sp, beg shell; (ch 1, dc in next dc) 8 times, ch 1, shell in next shell; ch 1, turn.

Row 4: Sl st in 2 dc and ch-2 sp, beg shell; ch 3, skip one ch-1 sp, (sc in next ch-1 sp, ch 3) 7 times, shell in next shell; ch 1, turn.

Row 5: Sl st in 2 dc and ch-2 sp, beg shell; ch 3, skip one ch-3 sp, (sc in next ch-3 sp, ch 3) 6 times, shell in next shell; ch 1, turn.

Row 6: Sl st in 2 dc and ch-2 sp, beg shell; ch 3, skip one ch-3 sp, (sc in next ch-3 sp, ch 3) 5 times, shell in next shell; ch 1, turn.

Row 7: Sl st in 2 dc and ch-2 sp, beg shell; ch 3, skip one ch-3 sp, (sc in next ch-3 sp, ch 3) 4 times, shell in next shell; ch 1, turn.

Row 8: Sl st in 2 dc and ch-2 sp, beg shell; ch 3, skip one ch-3 sp, (sc in next ch-3 sp, ch 3) 3 times, shell in next shell; ch 1, turn.

Row 9: Sl st in 2 dc and ch-2 sp, beg shell; ch 3, skip one ch-3 sp, (sc in next ch-3 sp, ch 3) twice, shell in next shell; ch 1, turn.

Row 10: Sl st in 2 dc and ch-2 sp, beg shell; ch 3, skip one ch-3 sp, sc in next ch-3 sp, ch 3, shell in next shell; ch 1, turn.

Row 11: Sl st in 2 dc and ch-2 sp, beg shell; shell in next shell; ch 1, turn.

Row 12: Sl st in 2 dc and ch-2 sp; (ch 3, dc, picot, 2 dc) in next shell; Finish off; weave in thread ends.

Second Pineapple

Row 1: Attach thread to next ch-8 sp, in ch-8 sp work, (beg shell, ch 3, V-st; ch 3, shell); ch 1, turn work

Rows 2 to 4: Work same as First Pineapple.

Row 5: Sl st in 2 dc and ch-2 sp, ch 3, sl st in first dc of shell on row 5 of pineapple on right, complete beg shell with dc, ch 2, 2 dc; ch 3, skip one ch-3 sp, (sc in next ch-3 sp, ch 3) 6 times, shell in next shell; ch 1, turn.

Rows 6 to 12: Work same as First Pineapple.

Make 5 more pineapples same as Second Pineapple.

Eighth Pineapple

Row 1: Attach thread to next ch-8 sp; in same sp work (beg shell, ch 3, V-st; ch 3, shell); ch 1, turn.

Rows 2 to 4: Work same as First Pineapple.

Row 5: Sl st in 2 dc and ch-2 sp, ch 3, sl st in first dc of shell on row 5 of pineapple on right; complete beg shell with (dc, ch 2, 2 dc); ch 3, skip one ch-3 sp, (sc in next ch-3 sp, ch 3) 6 times, shell in next shell, sl st in first dc of shell on Row 5 of pineapple on left of work; ch 1, turn.

Rows 6 through 12: Work same as First Pineapple. At end, finish off; weave in thread ends.

Pretty Pineapples

STITCH GUIDE

Beginning Shell (beg shell): In specfied sp work (ch 3, dc, ch 2, 2 dc).

Shell: In specfied st work (2 dc, ch 2, 2 dc).

Beginning Double Shell (beg d-shell): In specfied st work [ch 3, dc, (ch 2, 2 dc) twice].

Double Shell (d-shell): In specfied st work [(2 dc, ch 2) twice, 2 dc].

Picot: Ch 3, sl st in last st made.

INSTRUCTIONS

Ch 6; join with a sl st to form a ring.

Rnd 1: Ch 1, 12 sc in ring; join with a sl st in first sc.

Rnd 2: Ch 1, sc in join; *ch 6, sc in next sc; rep from * around; ch 3, join with a dc in first sc.

Rnds 3 and 4: Ch 1, sc in join; *ch 6, sc in next ch-6 sp; rep from * around; ch 3, join with a dc in first sc.

Rnd 5: Ch 1, sc in join; *ch 5, in next ch-6 sp work, (sc, ch 20, sc); rep from * around, sc in next sp, ch 20, join with a sl st in first sc. Finish off; weave in thread ends.

Rnd 6: Attach thread to any ch-20 sp, work beg shell in same sp; *ch 8, shell in next ch-20 sp, rep from * around; ch 8, join with a sl st in 3rd ch of beg ch-3.

Rnd 7: Sl st in dc and ch-2 sp, beg d-shell in same sp; *ch 6, d-shell in next shell; rep from * around, ch 6, join with a sl st in 3rd ch of ch-3.

Rnd 8: Sl st in dc and ch-2 sp, beg shell; *ch 3, shell in next ch-2 sp, ch 4**; shell in next ch-2 sp; rep from * around, end at ** on last rep; join with a sl st in 3rd ch of ch-3.

Rnd 9: Sl st in dc and ch-2 sp, beg shell; *ch 2, 6 dc in ch-3 sp, ch 2, shell in next shell; ch 3, sc over ch sts of Rnds 6, 7 and 8, ch 3**, shell in next shell; rep from * around, end at ** on last rep; join with a sl st in 3rd ch of ch-3.

Rnd 10: Sl st in dc and ch-2 sp, beg shell; *(ch 1, dc in dc) 6 times, ch 1, shell in next shell, in next shell work, (dc, picot) twice; (dc in dc, picot) 6 times, in next shell work, (dc, picot, dc)**, shell in next shell; rep from * around, end at ** on last rep; join with a sl st in 3rd ch of ch-3.

Rnd 11: Sl st in dc and ch-2 sp, beg shell; *ch 3, skip one ch-1 sp, (sc in next ch-1 sp, ch 3) 5 times; shell in next shell, (dc in next dc, ch 3, sl st in first ch, ch 1) 8 times, dc in next dc**, shell in next shell; rep from * around, end at ** on last rep; join with a sl st in 3rd ch of ch-3.

Rnd 12: Sl st in dc and ch-2 sp, beg shell; *ch 3, skip one ch-3 sp, (sc in next ch-3 sp, ch 3) 4 times, shell in next shell; ch-1, turn.

Rnd 13: Sl st in dc and ch-2 sp, beg shell; *ch 3, skip one ch-3 sp, (sc in next ch-3 sp, ch 3) 3 times, shell in next shell; ch-1, turn.

Rnd 14: Sl st in dc and ch-2 sp, beg shell; *ch 3, skip one ch-3 sp, (sc in next ch-3 sp, ch 3) twice, shell in next shell; ch-1, turn.

Rnd 15: Sl st in dc and ch-2 sp, beg shell; *ch 3, skip one ch-3 sp, sc in next ch-3 sp, ch 3, shell in next shell; ch-1, turn.

Rnd 16: Sl st in dc and ch-2 sp, beg shell; shell in next shell; ch-1, turn.

Rnd 17: Sl st in dc and ch-2 sp, ch 3; dc in shell, picot, 2 dc in next shell. Finish off; weave in thread ends.

To complete unfinished pineapples:

Row 1: Attach thread to shell on right-hand side of any incomplete pineapple, beg shell in same sp; *ch 3, skip one ch-3 sp, (sc in next ch-3 sp, ch 3) 4 times, shell in next shell; ch-1, turn.

Rows 2 through 6: Rep Rows 13 through 17.